DISCI
DIVINE
DIRECTION

in real time

MW01256785

BY JOSEPH W. WHITE

Discerning Divine Direction in Real Time

Trilogy Christian Publishers
A Wholly Owned Subsidiary of Trinity Broadcasting Network
2442 Michelle Drive, Tustin, CA 92780

Copyright © 2022 by Joseph W. White

Scripture quotations marked NIV are taken from the Holy Bible, New International Version®, NIV®. Copyright © 1973, 1978, 1984, 2011 by Biblica, Inc.™ Used by permission of Zondervan. All rights reserved worldwide. www.zondervan.com. The "NIV" and "New International Version" are trademarks registered in the United States Patent and Trademark Office by Biblica, Inc.™

Scripture quotations marked NLT are taken from the Holy Bible, New Living Translation, copyright © 1996, 2004, 2015 by Tyndale House Foundation. Used by permission of Tyndale House Publishers, Inc., Carol Stream, Illinois 60188. All rights reserved.

Scripture quotations marked NASB are taken from the New American Standard Bible® (NASB), Copyright © 1960, 1962, 1963, 1968, 1971, 1972, 1973, 1975, 1977, 1995 by The Lockman Foundation. Used by permission. www.Lockman.org.

All rights reserved, including the right to reproduce this book or portions thereof in any form whatsoever. For information, address Trilogy Christian Publishing Rights Department, 2442 Michelle Drive, Tustin, CA 92780.

Trilogy Christian Publishing/ TBN and colophon are trademarks of Trinity Broadcasting Network. For information about special discounts for bulk purchases, please contact Trilogy Christian Publishing.
Manufactured in the United States of America

Trilogy Disclaimer: The views and content expressed in this book are those of the author and may not necessarily reflect the views and doctrine of Trilogy Christian Publishing or the Trinity Broadcasting Network.

10 9 8 7 6 5 4 3 2 1
Library of Congress Cataloging-in-Publication Data is available.

ISBN: 978-1-68556-432-2
ISBN: 978-1-68556-433-9

DEDICATION

I dedicate this book to my precious wife, Trisha. You've walked this journey called life with me twenty-five years now. Looking back, it seems like we've been through it all. Just like the vows we made to each other back on our wedding day. The highest of highs, the lowest of lows and everything in between. It's been one wild ride!!! The best is yet to come!

Me, you, and Jesus.

To my three life-changing daughters, Hannah, Danielle, and Lauren. May you know, trust, and cherish the Lord and HIS voice as you have me and mine.

FORWARD
by Pastor Jim Reed

I have known Joseph White for sixteen years, starting with a trip from south Florida to southern Virginia that was memorable for all the wrong reasons! As we served the Lord together at New Life Community Church, I watched him live through many of the experiences he tells of in this book. I saw him take the huge steps of faith he encourages you to take, and I watched him learn to trust the voice of God more and more in his life and ministry.

In other words, this is not a book of theory. This is a book by someone who has paid the price to learn how better to hear from God and respond to Him in faith and obedience.

I know you will be challenged, blessed, and encouraged as you read Joseph's story. May you be inspired to hear and respond to the life-giving voice of God in your own life.

ACKNOWLEDGMENTS

My special thanks to Bobby Ferrell for your blood, sweat, tears, and long hours on the projects that you did in my stead, releasing me to work on writing this book.

My special thanks to Kay McDaniel for your labor of love in editing my manuscript.

My special thanks to Emily Reed Love for taking your time to read through offering a fresh eyes perspective.

My special thanks to Jon and Becky Rogerson along with Jon Taylor for your cover design ideas.

CONTENTS

INTRODUCTION

Write... Write... Write...

I kept hearing the word "write," both in my head and from people I knew to people I barely knew. I would mention the least little thing, and they'd say, "You need to write about that." Now, here's something the wisest man in the world warned us about: "the writing of many books is endless, and excessive devotion *to books* is wearying to the body." (Ecclesiastes 12:12) According to Google, there are around 150,000,000 books in the world today. Whereas I love reading one good book after another, between Solomon's warning and the number of books already out there, why another book? And of all people, why should I write it?

One author helped me answer that question when he said, "It may have been done or said by someone else. That's a distinct possibility. but it hasn't been done or said by you. It hasn't come through your unique flesh and blood, through your life, through your experience and insight and perspective."

Author Max Lucado added this powerful truth when he wrote, "You can do something that no one else can do in a way that no one else can do it." This makes what you and I do unique and needed in this world.

Before beginning the process of writing this book, a dear friend to my family Allison Spicer texted me this quote from Albert Einstein: "There comes a point in your life when you need to stop reading other people's books and write your own." Morgan Harper Nichols also helped to seal the deal for me when she shared this bit of advice: "Tell the story of the mountain you climbed. Your words could become a page in someone else's survival guide."

Finally, Revelation 19:10, states that "... the testimony of Jesus is the spirit of prophecy," and Revelation 12:11 states, "And they overcame him because of the blood of the Lamb and because of the word of *their* testimony..." So, without further ado, here's my story, with one life-changing testimony after the next.

PART I

Couldn't Be God, Could It?

It started on a Wednesday back in August 2010. A phrase kept popping into my mind. *Leave Now. Leave Now.* At first, I dismissed the thought totally, but then it happened again and again and yes, again. Some say three's a charm, but four days in a row, I couldn't get around it. *Leave Now!* But I don't want to! *Leave Now.* But I've been here for eleven years, and this is all my kids know. *Leave Now.* But I don't have a job lined up, and I don't have any money saved up. *Leave Now.*

The more I thought through it, the more it didn't make sense. That… *THAT*… *couldn't* be God… could it? I mean, come on. I'm married with three kids — girls, for that matter. (Yes, the statistics are right, in case you're wondering; they do cost more, but they're worth every single penny!!!) How am I going to provide for them? What are people going to think? Speaking of thinking, I can tell you right now what my wife is going to think, and that is that I am NOT thinking clearly. She's going to think I am losing my mind. I kept running through all the "When, Where, and How" questions, being the analytical thinker that I am. With all those questions, you would have thought that a very logical answer would be attached to at least one of them.

Sunday rolled around and being part of a church staff, I was at church most of the day. Monday was my typical day off. However, with that phrase continually coming to my mind, I said to Trisha, "Hey Babe, I've got to go to work tomorrow."

"Why? It's your day off."

"I know, I know, but I've got to get some clarity on something."
Understatement of the year!

First thing Monday morning, hoping to get some insights into
that annoying phrase that I wanted to leave now (no pun intended)
I took off for the church. When I pulled into the church parking
lot, I noticed that no one was there that day. To be honest, I was
thankful because I needed some alone time. I went straight to my
office, shut the door behind me, sat down in my comfortable black
office chair, and proceeded to ask God a question. "God, if that
was you telling me to Leave NOW, I need you to do something
SIGNIFICANT to confirm that it was INDEED YOU! Because
if that was YOU telling me to *LEAVE NOW*, I want to let you
know that I don't know what to do and I don't know where to
go. IF THAT REALLY WAS YOU, GOD, telling me to LEAVE
NOW, and yes, I realize I'm repeating myself, BUT I need YOU to
do something SIGNIFICANT to confirm to me beyond a shadow
of a doubt that that was INDEED YOU!!!

One of the books that I would frequently read was *Streams in the
Desert*. I had that with me that morning. As I reached to open it up,
I reminded God one more time, to make sure that He was listening.
"God, as I open this little black book, if that was YOU telling me to
LEAVE NOW, I need you to confirm beyond a shadow of a doubt
that that was INDEED you. Because as I've told you, I don't know
what to do and I don't know where to go!!!"

With that said, I opened the book to the devotional for the day
which was *August 23* and the first sentence that I read was:

August 23
    "By faith Abraham… obeyed and went, even
though he did not know where he was going."
(Hebrews 11:8)

Tears immediately filled my eyes. I knew in an instant that it really was God telling me to LEAVE NOW. After finishing the reading, I closed the book and said, "OH MY, OH MY, OH MY — GOD, that was you!!!"

… BUT …

NOW, WHAT?

Before we get to that, let me fill you in on a few other things that are vital to this story.

Eight Months Earlier

It was December 2009, and at the end of the year I typically find myself in evaluation mode, looking back and thinking ahead. The more I thought about 2010, the more a statement came to the forefront of my mind. *2010: The Year You Begin. 2010: The Year You Begin.* I love poems, and I love rhymes, but did you notice anything in particular about that phrase? Did it jump out to you the way it did me? *2010: The Year You Begin.* Begin? Begin WHAT?

The more I asked God, the more distant, and quiet He seemed. Besides telling a few people about it, nothing seemed to happen in connection with that statement until five months later.

During the first week of May, I was invited to go to the DRIVE Conference, a conference put on by Pastor Andy Stanley's North Point Community Church in Atlanta, Georgia. One of the guys that went with us, Tim, lived an hour away from Danville. The reason I mention that is because of what happened later in the month. As May was coming to an end, I received a phone call late one Thursday afternoon from my buddy Patrick Sheldon, another one of the guys who attended the conference.

He said, "Hey, is there any way you can get off early tomorrow to play in a Golf Fundraiser?"

I told him it should not be a problem, plan to count me in. I had to get permission from Pastor Jim to leave work early that day to play.

Upon arriving, I saw Tim. Later, as we were playing golf, Tim said to me, "Joey, I've been praying for you since the conference."

I said, "Thank you," thinking to myself, *He must have meant he was praying for my daughter, who had had an allergic reaction while we were in Atlanta, and for my wife, who had been struggling through a long illness.*

As I began updating him on my daughter and wife, he interjected, "I've been praying specifically for you."

"Oh, Okay. Well, thank you!"

As we finished dinner after playing 18 holes of golf, I found myself walking with Tim out to the parking lot. As we parted ways, I turned and said, "Thanks again for praying for me!"

He said, "Oh yeah, by the way, as I've been praying for you throughout the month, this phrase kept coming to my mind: "Joey is going to begin a ministry, and you're supposed to help."

Stopping in mid-stride, I about-faced and said, "WHAT??? What did you say?"

He said, "I believe God told me that you are going to begin a ministry, and I am supposed to help you." I started walking toward him, but before I could ask him the first question, he quickly interrupted me, "Sorry, Joey, but I don't have time to chat right now. I've got to leave, or I'm going to be late for something."

With that, he hopped into his vehicle and pulled off, leaving me standing there in the middle of that parking lot. As I stood there thinking to myself, this question kept coming to my mind. *What in the world was that??? Why would he say something like that, and then leave?*

The next day, another friend of mine Ed called and said, "Hey Joey, I would like to invite you and your family to join us at our beach house the second week of June, Wednesday June 9 – Saturday June 12."

I was already planning to take some time off from work, so I said, "Hey, that sounds GREAT! My girls, and especially Trisha, will be super excited to hear this — Beach Trip!" As I got off the phone, I immediately thought about another good friend, Josh Shelton, that lived in the area. I kept in touch with him periodically, I called him and said, "Hey, man, I'm going to be close to you that week — is there any way that we can connect?"

He said, "Yes," and then asked me if it would be possible to stay an extra night and attend church with him the next day.

After checking, I called him back. "Yes, we can stay an extra day. Can't wait to see you." As we were talking, he got excited as he realized we would be at his Church on Sunday, June 13, which just so happened to be Miracle Offering Sunday.

I said, "What is Miracle Offering Sunday?"

He said, "Once a year, our leadership team prays and asks the congregation to give a special offering for a particular project over and above our regular giving. Last year over $300,000 came in on that one Sunday."

Impacted, to say the least! I said, "Well, cool, I'm looking forward to it." Upon hanging the phone up, these words popped in my mind.

Give $100!

WHAT? Ah, I don't have an extra $100 just lying around. PLUS, that will be the last day of our family vacation, and we are already staying an extra day in a hotel room that was not in our budget for that matter. Not to mention the other overdue bills, my list could go on, but I will spare you the boring details. Well, let me add one more thing. I don't even go to that church, and it's a huge church. My little $100 isn't going to make any difference. That couldn't be God! But the phrase *Give $100* wouldn't leave.

Ever been there?

Later, I hesitantly mentioned it to Trisha. "Hey Babe, I believe God wants me/us to give $100 when we go to that church." I explained the significance of the day — being Miracle Offering Sunday and all.

Being an MK (Missionary Kid) from Brazil, she grew up in a family accustomed to living that way... whereas I am sure she was tempted to think, "WHAT? Have you lost your mind? Have you forgotten about all the extra bills we have to pay?" Just like I had been doing moments earlier. She just listened quietly and shook her head.

The beach trip with Ed and Angela Fitzgerald was an absolute blast, and as always, it went by waaaaay too fast!!! Sunday morning, we got up and drove to the church to meet my friend Josh. As we pulled into the church parking lot, it was confirmed. I was right in thinking this church was massive, and my $100 is not going to make a difference here at all. It will be a mere drop in the bucket!!! Praise and Worship were good, and on that day, they had a *Guest Speaker*. In the middle of his message, this *guest speaker* started down a "rabbit trail" for a minute. It started with this statement, "I understand that you all do not know me, BUT your Senior Pastor knows me very well... and he knows that I would never do this unless I felt strongly prompted by the Spirit." With that statement, he looked down toward the front where the Senior Pastor was sitting, and they both nodded to each other.

With permission given, the *guest speaker* said, 'I feel like I am supposed to share something with someone, and this may be your first time here. You may even be from out of town."

I was already taking notes that day, BUT this caught my attention because he was two for two... I turned to Josh, and we both made eye contact with eyebrows raised.

He proceeded to say, "I believe that God brought you here to tell you that over the next three months, GOD is going to lay a brand-new foundation for you! Go ahead right now, grab your bulletin and a pen and write down at the top of your bulletin today's date and calculate three months from now."

To which I wrote *June 13*, put a dash, and wrote *September 13* at the top right-hand corner of my bulletin. With that said, he returned to his printed notes, preaching away as if that had never happened. To say GOD had my undivided attention for the rest of the sermon would be a slight understatement.

I was laser beam focused on that *guest speaker's* word and his message, which both appeared to be custom designed for me. I had forgotten that it was Miracle Offering Sunday. After the sermon, the lead pastor stepped up to the pulpit. He invited everyone who was able to give to come forward.

But right before he released all of us, he said, "Let me pray over you first." He proceeded to pray this simple, short prayer: "For these, who are giving today, God bless them 100-fold!" With that, he released us to come. We had chosen to sit in the top balcony in the back row. I believe this was the first time that I ever walked down to the altar to give an offering. As I was walking down all those steps, I was doing some quick calculations in my mind 100 x 100 equals... hey, I don't know about you, but I'm really starting to like the sound of this guy's prayer.

After the service was over, we went to one of my wife's favorite restaurants, Chipotle, and ate lunch. After catching up with my friend Josh, the family and I packed into the car for our four-hour ride home to the big D: Danville, VA, that is.

More Back Story

Right before we left to go to the beach, I began one of those week-long vacation house projects, ripping up carpet, putting down a new floor, the whole nine yards. Being the NON-handy man that I am, I decided to try and do most of the project alone, quickly discovering that I was in WAY over my head. I did what any smart son would do, I called my wonderful Jim "The Tool Man" Dad for help (That's not a typo — his name is Jim, NOT Tim). Yes, I'm dating myself here.

Because I waited until the last minute, my dad, the one and only Mr. Jimmie William White, was unable to work out his schedule to perfectly fit into mine. I did not quite understand. I mean, give me a break, he's retired, he's got free time (totally kidding). I finally found a place in my heart to let him off the hook. He was willing to work pretty cheap, anyway. By which I mean *free*! That's what dads are for, right???

On with the story: Upon leaving for the beach, the project was incomplete. I was only going for four days, but my dad assured me that he would be able to finish the floor in the living room because a friend of mine named Chris Bradner was willing to stop by and help my dad out for a few hours.

Back to the drive home. After four hours of driving, we approached our driveway. I noticed several vehicles as we turned into the driveway. Along with the cars, there were dozens of people, waving, jumping up and down, and clapping with BIG smiles on their faces! My wife looked at me and said, "What have they done?" thinking that I was in on the surprise, which I wasn't.

My best friend Stephen White (brother from another mother) was holding up a video camera videoing the whole thing. Now remember, just four short days ago, my house was in unfinished project mode. But, as we walked in on this day, not only was the project that I had started completely finished, but something like a mini-Extreme Home Makeover had taken place. Almost each item in my house was brand spanking new. All my close friends had come together while we were gone and done (parts and labor included) a $10,000 makeover on our (from my perspective) already lovely home!

My kids were in awe! My wife was doing the ugly cry. Yes, I've got pictures, and yes, they are still all on Facebook to this day. I was almost without words. I just walked around with my mouth wide open. I could not believe all that they had gotten done in only four days.

After everyone left, I kept walking around in my "new" home in utter disbelief. The next day, I was behind my car, unpacking from the beach trip. Being a private crier, I broke down, humbled, and overwhelmed with gratitude.

Cue for Commercial: Giving

Talk about an answer to prayer!!! I understand it doesn't always happen just like this, especially this quickly. But do you remember the prayer that the pastor prayed over us just several hours earlier? "God, for everyone that is able to give today bless them 100-fold!" $100 x 100 = $10,000! GOD, You blew me away!!!

Over the next two and a half months, I kept thinking through the theme that I believe God had given me for the year 2010 — *2010: The Year You Begin.* Tim's statement that he shared with me after that golf fundraiser in the parking lot — "God told me that you were going to begin a ministry and that I am supposed to help you." Last but definitely not least, that "rabbit trail" message that the *Guest Speaker* at the Wave Church shared: that over the next three months, *June 13 – September 13*, God was going to lay a brand-new foundation for me." I kept thinking to myself, *What does all this mean, and what is that new foundation going to be?*

Then, there I was, it was on a Wednesday morning in August. It was my girls' first day back to school following the summer break, it began. Yes, the phrase. Yes, that one. Remember... *Leave Now. Leave Now.*

For four days in a row, August 18-21, 2010, I kept hearing it. I told my wife on Sunday as we were leaving church, "Tomorrow, I've got to go to work."

On Monday, August 23, as I mentioned earlier, I went to my office to gain clarity. And did I ever! Remember, I read from that devotional book *Streams in the Desert* and the first sentence that I read was "By faith Abraham... *obeyed and went, even though he did not know where he was going.*" (Hebrews 11:8) Tears had immediately filled my eyes. I knew in an instant that it really was God telling me to LEAVE NOW.

If that weren't enough, here's what else jumped out at me while I was reading that devotional:

> "And the steps of faith often lead to total *uncertainty*
> or even *darkness* and disaster, but the Lord will open
> the way and often makes the darkest of midnight
> hours as bright as the dawning of the day.
>> Let us move forth today, *not knowing or seeing*, but
> trusting.
>> Many an opportunity is lost while we deliberate
> after HE has said, 'Move!'"

Right before I left my office that day, I told the LORD, "Okay, that was You telling me to *Leave Now.* I got it. I do, I am going to leave. But! Will you do me this favor? Will you please confirm it throughout the rest of this week? That way, when I share this with Trisha, she will believe me, that it really is You!"

Here are a few of the things that jumped out at me through the rest of that week:

TUESDAY: The next day, I read this statement: "Fair weather faith is *no* faith at all."

WEDNESDAY: The verse that seemed to jump off the page at me was *"And without faith, it is impossible to please Him,"* (God) [Hebrews 11:6 NASB].

THURSDAY: Thursday night, I received a phone call from a friend that lived out of town. He asked me how things were going. I informed him of the most recent developments. I told him that it appeared God was telling me to leave New Life. He asked me how sure I was… to which I stated, "I am about 80% percent sure." He strongly encouraged me to go online that night and watch/listen to a message by a pastor named Francis Chan. I went online that night and listened to the message by Francis Chan in which he shared with his congregation how he was leaving. Wouldn't you know it, he shared that he was about 80% sure that he was supposed to leave! Tears just filled my eyes again and began to stream down my face.

FRIDAY: My friend Jimmy, the manager from the local Outback Steakhouse, invited me to play golf with him. On the 9th hole, he told me about a book that he had been reading. I asked him the title, and he turned and looked straight at me and told me, *"It's Okay to be the Boss."*

I said, "What did you say?"

He said, "That's the title of the book: *It's Okay to be the Boss."*

I recognize that it may sound strange to you, but when Jimmy looked right at me and said that title out loud, with all the things that had been happening over the last several months, for me, it was as if, God was speaking to me through Jimmy telling me, "Joey, It is not only okay to want to be the boss, it is okay to be the boss!"

SATURDAY: On Saturday, I felt drawn to drop by LifeWay Christian Book Store, with all these thoughts running through my mind:

1. OK, God, you gave me this theme for this year — *2010: The Year You Begin...*

2. According to Tim, you told him that I am supposed to start a ministry and that he is supposed to help.

3. You gave that Guest Speaker what appeared to be a custom-designed word just for me about the laying of a brand-new foundation between *June 13* and *September 13*, and *September 13* is just around the corner.

4. Then the four days in a row broken record: *Leave Now. Leave Now.*

5. And on top of that, the book title that Jimmy shared with me: that *It's Okay to be the Boss.*

With all of this swirling through my head, I went straight to the Church Growth section in LifeWay, where all the church planting books were. I assumed that's gotta be God, right? (More about this in Part II) I stood there looking at easily a hundred different books that I could pick. I said to the Lord — privately — "If there is a book here that is for me, would you please make it crystal clear, because there are dozens of books, and I don't want to waste my time reading any of them if it is not for me right now. Please God, make it crystal clear that it is *my* book."

With that request out there, I then noticed several books on the top left corner of the first section. I said to myself, "That book must have just come out because there were a lot of them."

I reached and pulled one off the shelf. The title got my attention immediately. The title was *Church in the Making: What Makes or Breaks a New Church Before it Starts*. Interesting title and that is a perfect subtitle — I would absolutely want to know the answer to that because I don't want to fail if that's what I'm supposed to do.

The front cover had a tree on it that reminded me of the doormat that my friends placed at our doorstep after they completed the $10,000 remodel of our home back in June. I flipped the book over and read the back cover, and it talked about doing things God's way, meaning organically. My wife had recently been switching almost every single thing in our house over to organic products (that stuff is expensive!).

Everything about this book had me captivated. Though I was unfamiliar with Ben Arment, the author, I was familiar with the guy that wrote the Foreword, Ed Stetzer. I had read one of his books on church planting several years earlier while I was living in Brazil. I remembered sharing with my wife, Trisha, that if God ever led us to plant a church, I would much prefer to do it the way he played it out in his book. I figured, "Hey, if he checks off on this guy, then I will read it." Pausing right before I opened the book, I breathed one more request.

"God, if this is *my* book, please make it crystal clear that it is indeed *my* book."

With that said, I opened the book to the Foreword by Ed Stetzer, and this is what I read:

"Red Rover is an interesting idea. School kids would stand in two lines facing each other and take turns yelling out, 'Red Rover, Red Rover, send *Joey* right over!' Then *Joey* would have to leave his line and run as fast and hard as he could to break through the other line. If unsuccessful, *Joey* had to remain in the opposing team's line, and then another child would be called to come over."

As I am sure you are well aware, but just in case you aren't, Ed could have selected any name in the entire world to insert into the Red Rover game, but he just so happened to have used *my* name three times in the first paragraph. After reading that paragraph, I closed the book, took a step back, and said, "Oh, my! For me, it could not have been more clear. God, you are soooo amazing!!!"

With excitement, I drove straight home, determined to read that entire two-hundred-page book that afternoon, and that is exactly what I did.

By the end of the day, I said to Trisha... "Hey Babe, we need to chat."

I shared with her each thing that had happened over the last week, one confirmation after the next. Still hardly believing what I was hearing come out of my mouth, I told her that we were supposed to leave the church that we had been part of for the last eleven years.

"I knew it was coming," was her first response! She then asked, "Where are we going?"

To which I said, "I don't know."

"Where are you going to work?"

To which I said, "I don't know."

After a short pause, she said, "I've been sensing that our time was drawing to an end."

Well, cool, that was a lot easier than I thought it would be. With that settled, the next day, to seal the deal, I told a close friend of mine that I was leaving, meaning, by telling someone else outside of my family that lived locally, it was like drawing a line in the sand and stepping over it.

The following day, I informed Pastor Jim, my Senior Pastor, of the most recent developments. We met and discussed everything, and in that meeting we set a tentative date scheduling my transition for Sunday, *October 31, 2010*. Since I did not have any place to go and no money saved up, I figured, "Hey, I could hang out here for another 2 ½ months." Or so I thought.

The next day, I had another rather concise confirming encounter with a dear friend of mine, Jerry Eakes. He was my #1 volunteer, indeed my right-hand man, while I was at New Life. He is one of the greatest servant-hearted people I've ever had the privilege of knowing in my life. Jerry lived almost an hour from New Life, but always went the extra, extra mile to help me whenever he could. For me, it was just another day where he showed up to help me do yet another project. After we finished the project, as was our custom, we hopped in his truck to go to eat at our regular hang out, San Marcos Mexican Restaurant.

As we were driving to the restaurant, Jerry asked me this question: "When are you leaving?"

I said, "What?"

He said, "When are you leaving?"

I said, "I don't know what you mean!"

He said, in a rather calm but very direct way "Yes, you do!"

With that I gave Jerry my best Arnold Jackson/Gary Coleman impersonation: "Whatchoo talkin' bout, Willis?" (from Diff'rent Strokes).

To which he quickly said, "You know *exactly* what I'm talking about! When are you leaving???"

It quickly started dawning on me that somehow (I don't know how, but somehow) he knew. BUT how? How in the world could he know? No one knew except my wife, Pastor Jim, and that one other friend, at that point. Yes, I realize GOD knew — HE's the one that started all this, but that's beside the point.

I said to Jerry, "Yes, I am leaving next month, but how do you know?"

He said, rather, matter-of-factly "Two weeks ago, I was in the woods, minding my own business, enjoying the outside as I typically do — when I heard this statement as clear as a bell in my mind — *Joey's leaving!*"

I followed by saying, "Did you hear anything else? Did God tell you where I'm going?"

"Nope, I only heard, *'Joey's leaving!'* That's it!"

A little gripped and yet encouraged, I said, "That's amazing!"

Over the next four days, when I thought it couldn't get more real, it did.

The Spirit of God faithfully informed me by placing this phrase front and center in my thoughts. Like a blinking light on the dash of your car, this phrase, *Leave Now, means to Leave NOW!*

"Ohhhh, you're telling me I can't stay through *October 31?*"

"That's correct, leave now!"

Each day the phrase seemed to blink faster and brighter in my mind. *Leave Now* actually means to do just that. *Leave Now.* When I couldn't hold it in any longer, while Jim and I were walking across the parking lot from the church building to the office, I shared with him the newest revelation that *Leave Now* meant to *Leave Now.* I told him, "Whereas I want to stay and thought I could stay through

October 31, the Spirit has made it abundantly clear to me that I am required to leave now."

Jim said, in light of that, he would begin calling the Church council members to see how quickly they could all meet. He wanted them to hear straight from the horse's mouth, as they say, that way we would all be on the same page during my transition. Being a small Church in a small town, with me up and leaving after having been there for over a decade and leaving with no specific reason and no apparent place to go, rumors might unnecessarily begin spreading. And that is the last thing any of us wanted.

At first, the council members could not all get together until Saturday September 18, but then something changed on their end, and they, not me, moved it up to Saturday, September 11. We met, and I shared, in general, some of the things that the Spirit had revealed to me since December 2009. After praying for me, one of the council members, Cindy Scearce, spoke up and said that she heard the Holy Spirit tell her to tell me this: "What you are about to do is God-led, but it is going to be a very challenging Job-like experience. Trisha is going to have an even more difficult time with it." She went on to say this. "Hang in there, because what is to come is going to be even more amazing than you can imagine." She also noted, "What you are being called to do is going to be hidden from you for a lot longer than you are expecting, and I mean a lot longer!!!"

Hmmmm!!!

The next day I shared in both services that I was leaving New Life, I said specifically that, "Today is my last official day on staff here at New Life."

One of my prayer partners, Suzanne Brown, came up to me in between services and said, "As you go, you are no longer to be called Joey, but you are now to enter into your Joseph Ministry."

"Okay." (Quietly thinking to myself, *Whatever that means.)*

Once a year, our church did a Sunday night service, called the Living Room, which ended up being that night. That evening, during service, we took communion, and during that part of the service, I told the Lord that I wanted to step into the next season with a clean slate. With that, I said to the Lord, "I want to *bury* everything that needs to stay dead and not carry any of it into this next season."

Right after that, I had one of my close friends come up behind me, and he whispered into my ear this question. "Is God giving you a new name?" To which I slowly looked up, remembering earlier what Suzanne had just told me about entering into my Joseph Ministry.

And I said hesitantly, "Y e s."

He said, "What is your new name?"

I said, rather slowly — "J o s e p h???"

He said, "That's right!" And walked off just a grinning.

Interesting. I have been called Joey my entire life, never Joseph... except by my grandma, Gloria Gosney, and she only used it when I was in trouble. As you can see, I was not too fond of being called Joseph, at all!

As I was sitting there soaking all of this in, I was blown away at how God was interacting with me in such a personal way. Though I'd been a Christian for decades and on staff as a pastor for several years, the last few months and especially the last few weeks, I had been experiencing *daily* interaction with God, unlike and more than ever before in my life.

Yes, I am aware that is supposed to be the norm, right? Especially for a pastor. Sadly, it had not been the case for me. At the end of the night, as I was thinking back through all that had happened, it just dawned on me that tomorrow was not just any old Monday but that it was none other than Monday, *September 13.* Three months to the day that that Guest Speaker had said God was going to lay a <u>brand-new foundation</u> for me. Remember, the council, not me, changed our meeting from September 18 to September 11.

June 13, 2010 – September 13, 2010. Oh my, Oh my, Oh my! Can you say it with me? "Oh my!"

The New Foundation

Monday morning, *September 13,* 2010, I woke up extra early filled with excitement and expectation, unlike any other time in my life. I opened my *Streams in the Desert* book, and this is the first thing that jumped out at me. Remembering what I prayed during communion the night before, I read this sentence, "Last night I *buried* yesterday's fatigue, and this morning I took on a new supply of energy." Remember, just less than twelve hours earlier, I had said to the Lord in that service that I wanted to *bury* everything that needed to stay dead. God once again had my undivided attention. As if that were not enough after finishing *Streams,* I picked up Oswald Chambers *My Utmost for His Highest.* Wouldn't you know it, the title of the devotion for that day was: "AFTER SURREN-DER — THEN WHAT?" I sat there with my mouth gaping open, utterly amazed — God, it was you. I am doing the right thing! Oh my, oh my, oh my! I really am hearing from You!

I could barely read the rest of the devotional. I just sat there in belief and still yet some disbelief. Don't get me wrong, I knew God was real, but I hadn't experienced Him like this, meaning this often and this consistently. To be accurate, I need to say, He was blowing my mind! It had never dawned on me, that this type of relationship was available.

On September 16th, 17th, and 18th, I had another, *Couldn't Be God* experience. I had a new phrase that began to crop up in my mind. Evidently, this was going to become a regular part of my life. The new phrase was: "*Pay off your building fund commitment!*"

WHAT ?

"*Pay off your building fund commitment! The one you made to New Life.*"

Ahhhhhhhhhhhh, that's TWO THOUSAND DOLLARS, GOD!!!! I don't have two thousand dollars! I quickly dismissed it because from my perspective, that couldn't be God!!! I know, I know, after all that had just happened, and the fact that I had been experiencing all of this stuff firsthand, no way should I still be this quick to question/doubt God. On top of that, the Church was getting ready to have a Card Shower for us Sunday to bless us financially as a final farewell. I started thinking through things and began to feel a little more confident that after being there for eleven years, surely more than enough money would come in to cover that. Whereas I did not want to do it, I figured, with all the other things that had happened over the last few months and weeks, I might ought to obey.

I informed Trisha of the news, and, well… let me just say that she most assuredly had other plans for that money. But being an MK (missionary kid), she came around. My wife is simply amazing!!! I wrote out that check for $2,000, and first thing Sunday morning before service began, I walked over and gave it to my good friend Steve Driskill, the Church's finance guy. He looked at the check and said, "Are you sure that you want me to deposit that check?" (Steve knew my financial situation).

I said, "No, I mean, yes, well, maybe, I think so. How about this? I'll let you know. On second thought, go ahead!! Well, before you do that, let me call you tomorrow morning and confirm one hundred percent."

That afternoon Trisha and I read through all the cards from the families that we had come to love over the years at New Life. They were deeply touching. I added up all the money and checked it twice (to find out who'd been naughty or nice, sorry, different story). As I was saying, I added up the money two to three times to confirm that the amount was accurate, it totaled up to $1,445. (The only reason I am sharing this figure is for you to be able to appreciate the full weight of the story.)

Back Story

My wife, Trisha, had been quite sick for the last few years with thyroid and auto-immune issues. At times she had been bedridden for days and occasionally weeks on end. All of that to say, I was the single breadwinner. Yep, I brought home the bacon, as they say. Furthermore, we had three life changing daughters Hannah, Danielle, and Lauren that lived at home, and on top of that, before stepping out of New Life, they were attending a private Christian school. The same one they had been attending since Preschool. All three were also involved in multiple sports: volleyball, basketball, and softball.

In view of those things, we were living paycheck to paycheck and, at times, were playing catch up, big time! With the money I had in my checking account and with my next check from New Life being my last, I did some quick calculating only to discover that I had just enough money to cover that $2,000 check. You know, the one I had just given to Steve earlier that day. When I factored in my next rent payment, that was going to bring my checking account to a zero balance. Then, there was my savings account… well, there's no need to mention that because that already had a zero balance. In laymen's terms, that meant I was going to be out of money almost immediately.

I knew I was going to need to get another job, but for crying out loud! I was hoping for at least a week or two off before starting that next job. First world problem, I know, I know. Slightly nervous, I informed Trisha of the updated facts. They were rather challenging to swallow. There was some awkward silence for the rest of the evening. Remember, she took at least three prescriptions each month. Her "security" was getting ready to be deposited tomorrow morning with no reservoir to pull from. I could tell that fear was beginning to set in. Being the glass half-full kind of guy that I am, I told her that I couldn't help but notice that, as I checked that card shower list, some families were not on the list that I felt confident would do something for us, eventually, hopefully.

The next morning was Monday. I called Steve a little after 9:00 a.m., knowing he would be at the church office, and told him to deposit that check for $2,000. We heard from no one that day, and as a result, my wife gave me plenty of space to be alone (that's my nice way of saying the silent treatment), Monday turned out to be a long, quiet day. It seemed like I could hear each second tick away on our wall clock.

The next day was Tuesday, September 21. I woke up early, and during my Bible reading in the New Testament, in the Gospel of Luke, chapter 4 verse 1, I read how Jesus was led into the wilderness to be *tested* for *forty* days. Remembering what Cindy, the council member, had said to me back during the council meeting about how that this was going to be a challenging Job-like experience, and since the forty days seemed to jump off the page at me, I wrote it down in my journal: Forty days of Testing. I then did some quick calculating on paper and discovered that forty days from September

21 was Sunday, *October 31*. Hmmm, *October 31*. That was interesting. Remember, *October 31* was originally going to be my last day on staff. It may mean nothing, but that was interesting, at least to me. This is what I wrote in my journal:

> *September 21 – October 31*, 40 days of Testing. (I placed an asterisk beside **October 31.)*

Shortly after finishing my Bible reading, I received a phone call from friends who were on "my" Card Shower list, but not on "the" Card Shower list, if you know what I mean. I started breathing in some hope! They were indeed one of the families that had not given, but I thought that they would at least do something, eventually. When I answered the phone, the guy on the other end said, "Hey, do you have lunch plans today?"

I said, "No, we do not."

He said, "You might have noticed that we weren't part of the card shower."

(Oh no, not me!) He went on to add that he and his wife wanted to give it to us personally. Hip, Hip! Hope becoming tangible is a beautiful thing! With excitement, I informed Trisha. I could tell, though she remained quiet, that she was cautiously optimistic. They invited us to meet them at the Texas Steakhouse for lunch.

After being seated in our booth, we began chatting, just some small talk at first, and then the wife started sharing how she and her husband had already agreed to give a certain amount to us and had actually already written a check out prior to the card shower, reiterating how they much preferred to give it to us in person. Continuing, she said, "This morning, however, God spoke to me clearly that we're supposed to do something different."

(A quick moment of sheer honesty... for a nanosecond, I allowed that word "different" that she used to be filtered through my mind with a negative connotation attached to it, but I quickly took that thought captive to the obedience of Christ and started immediately thinking positively and believing for the best.)

She insinuated that the revelation caused a little friction between her and her husband, who was sitting there with us. She then said, "Well, here is what the Lord told us to give you initially." With that, she pushed the check that she had already written out about a week before the card shower across the table, and with what seemed like great intentionality, she pushed it directly toward Trisha. Leaning over toward the check, Trisha and I both gasped as we saw the amount on it. That check was made out to the tune of two thousand dollars. The exact amount of our building fund commitment that I had just paid off yesterday. With that, Trisha broke down — you know — crying — yes, it was another beautiful, ugly cry. Sorry, no pictures this time. I am sitting there just thanking God, and I mean THANKING HIM!!! Thinking to myself, *God that REALLY was YOU telling me to pay that off. Oh My, Thank you. Thank you. Thank you!!!!*

After Trisha was able to regain her composure, the wife continued by saying, "That is the check that we had already written out days before the card shower, and here, (holding what appeared to be another check in her hand,) is what I heard the Spirit say to me this morning. Before I give it to you, I want you to know the figure on this check came to me even stronger than the other one." She pushed that second check across the table. It was written out for five thousand dollars. With that, I joined in with Trisha, and we both broke down crying. Indeed, this was a holy moment! We couldn't talk for at least a minute or two.

"Oh my, Oh my, Oh my — God, I know, I've already said it to you, but that was you telling me to do all those things… I already knew you were, but God you are sooooo amazing! I mean you are amazing!!!" I thought I had already been blown away, but nothing could compare to what I was currently experiencing at that moment.

After regaining our composure for the second time, our friend asked this question, "If you do not mind me asking, why do you think God told us to do that, (meaning the second check)?" She said, "We would really like to know because it caused a little bit of conflict between us today, and that doesn't typically happen, especially when it comes to giving." Only because we were such close friends and because each aspect was amazingly confirming and exact, did I precede to tell them the whole story of how God had led me to pay off our Building Fund Commitment of $2,000 *before* the card shower, and how even with the money that came in from the Card Shower, after all funds were deposited and withdrawn, it zeroed out our bank account and, with nothing in savings, that meant we had no money, period. They were blown away just like we were. To be used by God in such a specific and special way, they felt just as blessed by God by giving as we did by receiving. As we sat there in that booth, it was indeed a holy moment for all four of us. We were in awe of our good, good Father!!!

If the experience was not already over the top, right before we got up to leave, the husband opened up his wallet and pulled out all of his cash and handed it to Trisha and said, "This is for you. You are not to pay any bills with this; you are only allowed to spend this on yourself." He then turned to me and said, "Joey, that money's off-limits."

To which I replied, "Yes, Sir!" The cash totaled $700. Did I happen to mention to you that we were in awe of our good, good Father!!! I already knew in theory that God was Jehovah Jireh, but

I was experiencing HIM being my provider in a whole new way!!! Having knowledge of something and experiencing something firsthand at this level was beginning to wonderfully and radically change my entire way of thinking!!!

Two days later, September 23, I received a phone call from a friend inviting me to go on an all-expenses-paid Spiritual Retreat for 3 ½ days [September 30 – October 3]. I thought to myself, "This is a no brainer, because I don't know what I am supposed to do next and I don't have anything, and I mean *anything*, lined up. What better thing to do than get alone with God, my genuine provider, and let HIM provide some new insight & new direction regarding my future?" I gave my buddy an "I am pretty sure, tentative yes" answer. However, considering my most recent encounters with God, I told him I needed to wait until I did my "devotions" in the morning before I could give him the final okay.

The next morning September 24, I got up and began my reading. This was the question that I laid before the Lord: "Am I allowed to go or not?" Short, sweet and to the point. Right after asking the LORD that question, I picked up my *Streams in the Desert* devotional book, and here is what I read:

> "… a service of waiting.
>
> … there are not only times for action but times to refrain from action. Inspire me with the knowledge that a person may sometimes be called to serve by doing nothing, by staying still, or by waiting. And when I remember the power of Your "gentle" whisper. (I Kings 19:12 (Note: I had just finished reading a great book entitled: *The Power of a Whisper*!!!)

I continued reading and remember, the question I asked the Lord was, "Am I allowed to go or not?" Here is what I read next. "I will not complain that sometimes the Spirit allows me NOT TO GO."

I don't know if I have ever read a sentence structured that way. It is like asking your parent, "Hey, can I go?" and your mom says, "Yes, your dad said that you are allowed not to go."

"What?" Come on, that couldn't be God telling me not to go on an all-expenses-paid Spiritual Retreat when all I have is time and all I need is insight and direction from HIM?

Could it?

Believe you me, I did not understand at that time why I was not allowed to go, but one thing was becoming more and more certain. After asking God that specific question and then to read what I just read, even though I did not have an answer to "WHY?" if I was ever sure about something, I was 100% sure that I was not allowed to go on this retreat.

Knowing I love poems, our good, good Father used one to cap it all off for me. As if I needed anything else, He gave me this poem:

> When I cannot understand my Father's leading,
> And it seems to be but hard and cruel fate,
> Still, I hear that gentle whisper ever pleading,
> God is working, God is faithful, *ONLY WAIT*.

After reading that, I immediately picked up my phone to call my friend to inform him of the news. He, like me, was dumbfounded and wanted to know WHY? To which I said, "I do not understand why. I only know that I am not allowed to go this time."

Within minutes of hanging up the phone, another buddy, who had gone WAY OUT OF HIS WAY, pulled into my driveway, having driven forty-five minutes to hand-deliver last-minute paperwork that they had had to pull some strings to get for me to be able to go to that retreat at the last minute. I quickly informed him of the news, "Hey, man, I am sorry to tell you this, but I am not allowed to go."

"Why not," he asked?

"Hold on a second, and I'll let you know." To which I ran into the house, grabbed my journal, and came back outside to his truck and read to him what I had just read minutes before.

With that my friend said, "Well, Okay. You best obey!"

I know I haven't mentioned this, but I was beginning to realize, unlike any other time in my life, that God is the Perfect Communicator!!!

Monday morning, September 27, I woke up and, as usual, began my reading. However, I made one small change. I decided to read from a different Bible translation. I typically would read out of my NASB (New American Standard Version), but this morning I picked up my NLT Bible (New Living Translation) and continued my Bible reading plan for the day, which started in the Old Testament with the book of Haggai. This translation is dated like we date things nowadays. Other translations date like this, "on the third day of the fourth month." For some reason, while I was reading, the only thing that jumped out at me were these dates: August 29 / September 21 / October 17 / December 18.

These were all meaningful in the book of Haggai, and what was interesting to me is that two of the dates were significant for me as well, and they had just recently occurred in my life. Haggai 1:1 reads: "On *August 29...*" If you recall, for personal accountability, I shared with someone local other than my wife that God was telling me to leave New Life.

Haggai 1:15 reads: "...on *September 21...*" Two things of significance happened that day:

1. 40 Days of Testing – *September 21 – October 31* (Remember *October 31* was going to be my last day on the job at New Life)

2. Dear friends gave us those two checks, one for $2,000, the exact amount that I had written to pay off our building commitment, basically zeroing out my account and one for $5,000 and then handed Trisha $700 cash to spend only on herself.

The other two dates were:

- Haggai 2:1 reads: "Then on *October 17...*"
- Haggai 2:10 reads: "On *December 18...*"

With all four dates being of importance in the book of Haggai and with the first two also being recently significant in my own life, I took the time to write out all four dates in my journal like this: *August 29 / September 21 /* October 17? December 18? 4 Exciting Dates from Haggai 1- 2.

Taking into account the first two dates being recently significant, I could not help but wonder if this was God's way of telling me that the other days were also going to be substantial for me... we shall see!?!?!?!

On Thursday of that same week, September 30, I felt prompted to stop by LifeWay Christian Bookstore. With all these things jumping out at me during my daily devotions, I was eager to see what was next. I went up one aisle, and down another, then, there it was, seemingly crying out for me to pick it up: the book entitled: *Walking with God* by John Eldredge. The subtitle is what grabbed me: "Talk to HIM. Hear from HIM. Really."

I couldn't pay for the book quickly enough. For me, that is what I had been experiencing, unlike, and more than, ever before in my life. As I hopped in my car, it started pouring down rain. Being super excited, I just started reading the book right then and there. However, above the noise of the water pounding on the car, I started hearing something over toward my left. As I turned and looked, the only thing I noticed was a young lady in the car beside me, and she was leaning forward with her head up against the steering wheel. She was crying... well, more like sobbing. This thought popped in my mind.

"Go pray for her!"

"What?! It's raining! On top of that, she's a female, and she'll think I'm a creeper, that I'm trying to hit on her, or that I'm stalking her. She needs a woman to pray with her."

"Go pray for her."

"I can pray for her right here in the car, plus it's raining harder now!"

"Goooo... pray for her!"

I want to say that after all of the most recent whispers and holy moments that I'd been experiencing, that I quickly jumped out of my car, into the pouring rain and gently knocked on her door. Upon her cracking the window, I began telling her I could hear her crying and wanted to make sure she was okay, and that I would pray for her if she were willing. I want to say all of that. But that would be a big fat lie!

As I sat there, wrestling with this most recent phrase in my head: *Go pray for her*, she cranked her car and pulled away. To which,

I'm sitting there thinking to myself, *Oh well, whereas I missed that one, I will at least pray for her right now as she drives away.*

As I started my prayer, my prayer was abruptly interrupted by this phrase: *"Follow her."*

Now that obviously couldn't be God telling to stalk a damsel in distress.

"Follow her!"

"Nooo waaay!!!"

As she pulled away, she turned into the intersection and proceeded to — of all things — park. Yes, you read that correctly. She parked herself right there in the middle lane. Now here's the thing, where she stopped just so happened to be the busiest intersection for this particular shopping center. You don't park in that middle lane. But wouldn't you know it, the entire time she sat there, not one single car came to turn. Meanwhile, I am the innocent bystander here, just sitting here trying to mind my own business watching.

As she sat there... and sat there... no other car came, and I continued to hear that phrase over and over in my mind. I couldn't believe it could be from God.

"Follow her."

Finally, since she was apparently waiting for me to follow her, I reluctantly cranked my car to begin tailing her, from a distance. (Shout out to Bette Midler.) You guessed it — as if being perfectly cued by someone else (I wonder who that could be), right as I made my approach, she pulled off, and the tailing began.

She drove from LifeWay, across town to the Kmart Parking lot. I pulled in, and, as I parked a few spaces away, yes, I heard it again: *"Go pray for her."*

I got out of my car this time, and yes, it was still raining. She had those window guards, thus allowing her to crack the window, blocking the rain from getting in. She was still crying. Noticing the window cracked, I carefully (actually, a better word would be *nervously*) proceeded to walk up to her door and knock on her window. After introducing myself, I began to tell her the entire long-drawn-out story. For those inquiring minds that want to know, her name was Emily (well, not her real name), she was from a neighboring state and had just experienced a severe heartbreak. I took the time to pray with her, assuring her GOD was going to watch over her and allow the healing process to begin.

Driving home, I began repenting of how self-centered I had become in such a short period. You see, whereas I was excited and blown away by all my new personal experiences that I had been thoroughly enjoying, I had quickly gotten distracted and had forgotten about others. But God, in His goodness, had parked that brokenhearted young lady right beside me, right after I purchased that book that I believe I was led to purchase, with such a fitting title, *Walking with God* by John Eldredge, with that custom-designed subtitle: Talk to HIM. Hear from HIM. Really.

Was I ever hearing from HIM! I REALLY was (and still am to this day).

And so can you for that matter! Really!!!

Having an abundance of time, I did a lot of reading and writing down all the things that seemed to jump out at me. For example, *Isaiah 6:1-2 NASB*, which reads:

> "The Spirit of the Lord God is upon me,
> Because the LORD has anointed me
> To bring good news to the afflicted;
> He has sent me to bind up the brokenhearted,
> To proclaim liberty to captives
> And freedom to prisoners;
> To proclaim the favorable year of the LORD

And the day of vengeance of our God;

To comfort all who mourn,"

There were other scriptures, too, like *Luke 4:17-20*, where Jesus quotes these verses from *Isaiah 61*, as well as *Matthew 25*, which focuses on the standard by which we will all give an account when we stand before God. These passages had been popping up all over the place. Although I had been in ministry most of my adult life, when faced with these passages, I will have to say my life did not reflect what these passages revealed. But with all these new experiences, it appeared God had fruitful plans in store for me.

During this time frame, I was also invited to participate in a ministry called Kairos Prison Ministry. I went to my first Kairos Prison Ministry Training on Saturday, October 2. Throughout the day, I experienced one confirmation after another that I was certainly supposed to be there. That afternoon, while driving home, I sensed that I was not to return to New Life for Sunday's church service. But I had no clue as to where I was to go to church.

Late Saturday evening, I found myself in Walmart purchasing something for Trisha, when I bumped into my old friend Patrick Sheldon. He came right out and asked me, "Hey, where are you going to church tomorrow?"

To which I said, "I don't know, but I don't think I am supposed to go to New Life. Why do you ask?"

He said, "Why don't you come with us?"

"Where are you going?"

"We're going to visit Tim's church in Greensboro."

Tim, I hadn't seen or spoken to Tim since that golf tournament back in May. (Remember, Tim is the guy that shared with me that God had told him that I was going to start something and that he was supposed to help.)

"Count me in… What time do I need to be prepared to leave?"

He said, "Be ready by 9:00 am. I'll swing by and pick you up."

The next morning, Sunday, October 3, we traveled to Greensboro, N.C. to Daystar Church, about an hour away. The music was excellent and, guess what else they had? They had none other than a *guest speaker* that Sunday. At the end of the message, the *guest speaker* said that he felt prompted at the very last minute to show this clip from a TV show called *Criminal Minds*. He added that it was from the episode from this past Wednesday night.

Before I share with you the contents of that clip, know this. I had just been asking the Lord another important question:

"Lord, do you want us to return to New Life and continue serving You there? Or do we go somewhere else, and if we go somewhere else, are we allowed to let Hannah, our oldest daughter, still attend New Life separately because of the Youth Group?"

My question boiled down to this: Does leave mean to leave the staff, or does leave mean to leave altogether?

Background

In the TV Show *Criminal Minds*, JJ, a member of the staff, is leaving the organization she has been with for many years. (Remember, I had just left New Life after being there for eleven years.) With that question on the forefront of my mind, here is the clip from *Criminal Minds* that the *guest speaker* shared.

JJ speaking, word for word:

> "I'm thankful for my years spent with this family. For
> everything, we've shared. Every chance we had to
> grow. I'll take the best of them with me and lead by

their example wherever I go. A friend told me to be honest with you. So here it goes —

This isn't what I want, but I will take the high road. Maybe it's because I look at everything as a lesson or because I don't want to walk around angry or maybe it's because I finally understand — there are things we don't want to happen but have to accept — things we don't want to know but have to learn — and people we can't live without, but have to let go."

As I sat there in that pew. I couldn't believe my eyes and ears. Did I just see and hear what I thought I saw and heard?

I realize this goes without saying, but to me, the answer was crystal clear: Leave meant to let go and leave entirely, and so we did.

Special Note: Remember that invitation that I received from that friend to go on that all expenses paid Spiritual Retreat from Thursday, September 30 – Sunday, October 3. If I would have, from my perspective, disobeyed and went, I would have not gone to LifeWay and purchased John Eldridge's book entitled *Walking with God: Talk to Him. Hear from Him.* Really when I did. I would have missed out on that turning point encounter with God and "Emily" (not her real name), that brokenhearted young lady from that neighboring state. Furthermore, I would have missed out on my first Kairos Training Session. And last, but definitely not least, I would have missed out on God's very creative "last minute" custom-designed answer to my question through yet another *guest speaker's* Holy Spirit prompting. As a result of all of these events, here is what I wrote down in my journal:

When all signs appear to be giving you green lights to go, please be sure and listen with both ears because what seems to be a definite GO may be an absolute NO.

On Friday, October 7, a friend of mine called my home phone and said, "Hey, can you meet me for lunch?"

I said, "Sure thing."

As we ate, he shared with me that the Lord told him to purchase me a cell phone. The reason that is so significant is because upon leaving New Life, not only did I turn in all my keys, but I also turned in my cell phone. Having no home phone meant I had no way of communicating unless someone dropped by the house. He ended up getting me the latest, greatest smartphone with unlimited data — so cool!!! Jehovah Jireh, which means in case you don't know = The Lord Will Provide, Genesis 22:14, NASB.

A little over a week later (Saturday, October 16) while driving home from the Saturday Kairos Training Session, I started having this sense that I was supposed to do something, but I wasn't quite sure what it was. The closer I got toward home, the more I sensed that we were not supposed to go to Daystar the next day with our friends. Even though services had been "fantabulous" and they had been such a blessing, something was up!

When I got home, after a few odds and ends, I opened up my laptop and started surfing the world wide web, eventually landing on North Point Community Church's website. One of the first things that popped up on their site dealt with small groups. These two letters seemed to jump off the screen at me, C3. They reminded me of a conversation that I had had months earlier with a friend. While we were chatting, he mentioned to me, as if in passing, "Hey, Joey, if you're ever in the Greensboro area on a Sunday, you should go check out this Church called C3. It's really cool."

That is all I remembered him saying. Now here is the neat thing: while this months-old conversation was running through my mind, my middle daughter Danielle runs in from playing basketball outside, and of all the things that she could have said to me, the first thing out of her mouth were these words,

"Hey Daddy, I thought you said that when we left New Life that we were going to visit other churches, too."

Looking at here with a big smile on my face, I said, "You're exactly right." Pointing to my computer screen, I said, "This is the one that we are going to visit tomorrow: C3 in Greensboro, NC."

Although we had been going to Daystar with all our other friends and thoroughly loving it, with those back-to-back occurrences, I knew we were supposed to go to C3 Church the next day. Not that I was attempting to get them to follow me, but none of my friends agreed with me, and that included my wife and my oldest daughter Hannah.

Because we had to pass Daystar to get to C3 that day, there was ample opportunity for several innuendos to be shared with the hopes of changing my mind at the last minute. They laid it on thick, let me tell you!

As we successfully pulled into C3 Church's parking lot, we were greeted by a friendly parking attendant. He said,

"Is this your first time?"

I said, "It sure is."

He said, "You're going to love our Church," he continued, "and you couldn't be here on a better day, because today we have a *guest speaker*, and she is amazing."

On the exact Sunday that God directed me to break away from my friends and go to this other Church that I'd never been to before, that was at least thirty minutes further, it was significant that they would have none other than a *guest speaker*. This *guest speaker* spoke on David and Goliath, with the focus on overcoming your Goliath. More specifically, she said, "If you do not kill your Goliath, you will be overwhelmed with fear and never fully enter into all that God is calling you to do."

My wife Trisha will tell you that overcoming fear had been a considerable part of this entire process for both of us. We were supposed to be there for that message beyond a shadow of a doubt! As I listened, I was thinking to myself, *This message is so custom designed that we could be in here all by ourselves.*

Ever been there?

After getting home from C3, I took a long Sunday nap. Later that evening, as my girls were doing their homework, I went back onto North Point Community Church's Website to watch their service. That day they were kicking off a new sermon series entitled "Game Plan" with the perfect subtitle. (Drum roll, please.) The subtitle is: "Discover God's Will for Your Next Step." More precisely, in the area of your career.

That sermon series would prove to be on time for me. Each sermon seemed to be written just for me. At the end of that day, I wrote these things down:

> "Leaving the comfort zone of our friends and a remarkable church to obey another direction, the confirmations of a *guest speaker* and the topic of fear which was absolutely a stronghold in our lives which needed to be broken, and then to arrive home and have North Point kick off a sermon series that addressed the very thing that I needed an answer to 'What am I supposed to do next?' Wow!"

Special Note: All of that happened on *October 17*, which by the way ended up being the 3rd of the 4 dates that jumped out at me from my reading in the Old Testament book of Haggai.

Remember, August 29 / September 21 / *October 17* / December 18?

As I am sure you would be, I was now very, very intrigued about *December 18*? Wondering??? What significance that date would have for me? We shall see…

As you continue reading see if your Sherlock Holmes, Perry Mason, Ben Matlock-like observational skills detect the new but not exactly wanted repetition I'd been encountering.

Ready?

On October 19, while I was writing down all that had jumped out at me. Here is what I wrote down from my reading from *Streams in the Desert*:

"He (God) will provide sufficient evidence to confirm it beyond the slightest doubt."

"God wants us to act only once we have HIS mind in a certain situation."

"… we are to listen, and also examine His providential work… in order to glean the full mind of the Lord." A.B. Simpson

"As long as that way is hidden, it is clear that there is no need of action, and He holds Himself accountable for all the results of keeping you exactly where you are. *Selected* For God, through ways we have not known, will lead His own."

On October 23, I was out and about, and I ran into somebody that I knew, and they just so happen to make a comment about *my hair turning gray.* When I got home, I sat down to do some figuring regarding our bills and the money in our account, or should I say the lack thereof. Later, I settled down to do some extra reading, and I came across this poem, *Streams in the Desert:*

> "If after toiling,
> *Your wealth should fly away*
> And leave your hands all *empty,*
> And *your hair is turning gray.*
> Remember then your Father
> Owns all the sea and land;
> Blessed are you if you trust
> When you cannot understand."

This poem reminded me of one of my devotional readings from earlier in the month. I Kings 17:7 (NIV) "Some time later the brook *dried up,*" The other parts that jumped out at me while I was reading through that devotional from *Streams in the Desert* on October 5 were as follows:

> "The education of our faith… the material insecurities
> of life that cause our lives to be spiritually established.
> … we must all learn the difference between trusting in
> the gift and trusting in the Giver.
> And whenever our earthly stream or any other
> outer resource has *dried up,* it has been allowed so we
> may learn that our hope and help are in God," F.B.
> Meyer

Special Note: As I was writing out that last sentence, my pen actually *ran out of ink*, forcing me to get another one to finish.

Are you beginning to notice anything?

God appeared to be using every means at HIS disposal to get my undivided attention. Was I ever getting ready to learn the truth of that!

Remember, at this point, whereas I had been asking God what to do next in almost everything I did, I still had not worked for money since I had stepped out from New Life. Primarily, because I never heard him direct me to, and secondly, I had money in my account to take care of my bills, plus some, at least until now.

I was beginning to get a sense that God was preparing me through repetition for something altogether new, but I would have never guessed what HE had up His sleeve. With my finances starting to run out and sensing I had no direction regarding work, I began to explore other options. I thought to myself, "Hey, I can pull all the money out of my small retirement fund and live off that for the rest of the year, until I get a clear direction."

I decided to call a few wise guys, and they all said, "Don't do it." I then picked up a book by Dave Ramsey, another wise guy, and he said the same thing. I put that book down a little frustrated, because I wanted to cash in that 401K to give me some more time. Walking over to the TV, I clicked it on, and in rapid succession, as the anointed channel surfer that I am, started flipping channels. (Trisha doesn't exactly like it when I have the remote in my hand.) While flipping the channels, I stopped for just a second, and I kid you not, the guy on that channel was talking about finances. Here is what proceeded out of his big mouth. He said, "*If you have a retirement fund, don't you dare cash it in and try to live off of it!!!*"

What? "Did he really just say that out loud?"

Sitting there, I quickly went from being frustrated to stunned. I could hardly believe my eyes and ears. Considering the repetition, I knew immediately that I could not go through with it. In case you weren't following closely enough, I remind you to remember, all of this happened literally within a matter of minutes of each other.

I called my friends the wise guys, and they both said no.

I hung up the phone and reached for Dave Ramsey's book, and he said no.

And then, while doing what I do best with a remote, that other financial guru yelled at me through my own TV screen, screaming, *"If you have a 401K, don't you dare cash it in and start living off it!"*

I was running out of money, again with nothing lined up, and here was God going the extra mile, again to ensure I do something. But what that was exactly was still eluding me. I don't know if I've mentioned this before, but God is the Perfect Communicator! I don't know about you, but I was beginning to notice a pretty significant pattern with all this perfect communicator stuff – He has this particular tendency about Himself, and that tendency is to keep on repeating Himself.

Ever noticed that about Him?

I was approaching the end of October, and, if you will remember initially, *October 31* was going to be my last day on staff at New Life. Back on September 21, if you recall, I read about Jesus being tested for forty days – since that was what jumped out at me during my reading, I wrote it down because I sensed the Lord say to me, *"The next 40 Days you will be tested."*

Remember my journal entry: *September 21 – October 31 = 40 Days of Testing.*

With the 31st steadily approaching, which was the end of the *40 Days of Testing*, I was intrigued and hoping to be relieved from this test.

Early Sunday morning, *October 31*, God was for sure getting my attention about something unexpected to say the least. Here is what I wrote down in my journal after reading from Mark 8:17-21:

Why are you so worried about having no food?

Won't you ever learn or understand?

You have eyes — can't you see?

You have ears — can't you hear?

Don't you remember anything at all?

What about the 5,000 I fed with five loaves of bread?

How many baskets of leftovers did you pick up afterward? 12

And when I fed the 4,000 with seven loaves, how many large baskets of leftovers did you pick up ? 7

Don't you understand even yet?

"Evidently NOT!!!"

That day we went to Daystar Church in Greensboro again, and Tim invited us and some other friends over for lunch after church. While there, we had a great time, and people were asking me, "Joey, what's next?" To which I had to admit I felt still entirely in the dark. I shared that it was like there was *a cloud over my head. I had no answer!*

After lunch was over, everyone seemed to naturally break up into groups just chatting. As was my habit, I walked over to the bookshelf and started looking at all the books. One book caught my attention immediately. It was entitled *48 Days to The Work You Love*. That's a different title than I'm used to seeing on a book. I had never heard of the author, but the foreword was by Dave Ramsey. If Dave backed him, he must be worth reading. I immediately turned to read Dave's foreword and then the Introduction. At the end of the Introduction, here is what I read on Page 5: "Believing that God created me for His purpose and scheduled every day of my life, I commit the next 48 days to new clarity and a plan of action for moving into God's calling for me."

Below that paragraph was a place to sign my name and write in today's date as an act of commitment on my part. Once I calculated 48 days from *October 31*, I couldn't believe my eyes at first. There it was in black and white, yes, the 4th significant date. Remember my reading from the Old Testament book of Haggai:

August 29 / September 21 / October 17 / *December 18?*

Joseph W. White October 31 – *December 18*

I was utterly beside myself and started interrupting everybody's conversations, telling them what had just happened. Someone spoke up and said, "What does that mean?"

I said, "I don't know, but I don't care, because it's the fourth date! It's the fourth date — can you believe it?"

For them it was like, "We don't have a clue what you're talking about, but we're happy that you're happy!"

Boy, was I ever happy. WOW! Can you believe it?!?! WOW, GOD, WOW!!!

The next day Monday, November 1, I received a phone call around 10:00 a.m. from my good friend Ed Fitzgerald. He said, "So, yesterday was October 31, the end of the 40 Days of Testing. I waited as long as I could to call, I just have to know — what did the Lord tell you? What's next?"

I said, "Well, Ed, I feel pretty confident. However, I have not finished my morning devotions. Let me do that first, and I will give you a callback." I got off the phone and went straight into the living room and opened my devotional book, *Streams in the Desert*, to November 1. Here are the words that I read with my own two eyes:

"When *the cloud* remained... the Israelites... did not set out. (Numbers 9:19, NIV).

When God sends *no answer*, and '*the cloud remain*[s],' we must wait. HE never keeps us at our post without assuring us of His presence or sending us daily supplies.

Young person, wait — do not be in such a hurry to make a change! Minister, stay at your post! You must wait where you are until *the cloud* begins to move. Wait for the Lord to give you His good pleasure! He will not be late!" from Daily Devotional Commentary.

Do I even need to remind you of what came out of my mouth just a little over twelve hours earlier, while I was at Tim's house? When being asked by all my friends, "So, Joey, what's next?"

Remember, I said, "... I have to admit I still feel totally in the dark." I shared that it was like there was *a cloud over my head. I had no answer!*

And if the answer were not already clear enough, our heavenly Father, being the perfect Father that He is, and knowing how much I enjoyed poems, included this poem to cap it all off: An Hour of Waiting!

Yet there seems such need
To reach that spot, sublime!
I long to reach them — but I long far more
To trust HIS time!

"Sit still, My children" —
Yet the heathen die,
They perish while I stay!
I long to reach them — but I long far more
To trust HIS way!
It's good to get,
It's good indeed to give!
Yet it is better still —
O'er breadth, through length, down depth, up height,
To trust HIS will!

F.M.N.

The answer seemed abundantly clear to me that I was to keep doing what I had been doing and keep waiting and preparing for at least forty-eight more days!!!

I called my buddy Ed back, and I said, "Forty-eight more days."

He said, "Great! Forty-eight more days — that's great! — I'll be praying!!"

That first week of November 2010, I had several loose ends to tie up. During that week, I received a phone call from a friend, and he invited Trisha and me to a weekend Marriage Retreat, all expenses paid, Friday through Sunday evening. Trisha and I both felt that we were supposed to go. I took time again to do some more calculations and discovered that by next week, I would be practically out of money once again. I shared with a couple of my closest friends that I needed for them to partner with me in prayer, asking for crystal clear divine direction considering my financial situation, though not giving them any specifics.

I sense what might be rolling around back there in the recesses of your mind. Don't worry, I heard my wife say it over and over and yes over again — "Go get a job! Duh!"

However, with all that had happened, I just wanted God to tell me specifically. I know. He already has, in the B I B L E (yes, that's the book for me). Just go look it up, it's right there in black and white! Let me help you, help me. 2 Thessalonians 3:10 reads: "If you don't work, you don't eat!" It seems pretty clear from scripture that I should simply go and get a job!!! Period. Right?

Let's keep reading. I told my friends that I would decide by Monday night, November 8, as to what I would do regarding work.

We went to the Marriage Retreat and had a wonderful time. Upon arriving home on Monday, November 8, I received a phone call from one of my accountability partners, Josh Barrett. He wanted to know if it would be okay for him to stop by the house.

I said, "Sure."

Within an hour, he was at my home. When he got out of his car, he cut straight to the point by asking me this question: "So, what do you feel the Lord wants you to do regarding work?"

I told him, Trisha is struggling with what I am feeling lead to do, but because of all the repetition that I've been receiving during my quiet time, I told him that I felt the Lord wanted me to continue living by faith and trusting Him to speak to people at just the right time to take care of my family. Just like he had been, since leaving New Life back in September.

To which he said, "That's great, because I feel the same way and here's why."

You're going to absolutely love this story... are you ready?

He said, "Late Friday evening while you were at your Marriage Retreat, I grabbed my cell phone and typed out this message to send you through text: 'Joey, praying for you. Listen, I believe God has something very special for your marriage at this retreat. So enjoy, and when you get back home, go get a job.' Before sending that text message, I prayed this little prayer. 'God, if you want Joey to go get a 'regular' job when he gets back from that Retreat, then be sure that he receives this text message tonight.'"

"After praying that simple, little prayer," he said, "I pushed send, and it did not go through, so I pushed send again, and then again. However, the red X remained, indicating that the message had failed to go through." He said, "I waited a few minutes and tried again, and yet again, each time, the message would not leave my phone. Over the next 20-30 minutes, I tried to send that text message to you about two dozen times, and it would never leave my phone."

He then pulled out his phone and showed me the message and the red X.

To which I said, "That's AMAZING!!!"

Whereas, I had already made my decision, that was a pretty cool confirming story with visuals and all. I said, "Hey, before you leave, do you mind doing me a HUGE favor? Would you go into the house and share with Trisha what you just shared with me?"

Trisha was, let's say, moved by the story, but not as amazed as I was.

Interestingly enough, I noticed that November 8 – December 18 was another forty-day period — more repetition. During the month of November, I found out that several guys I knew were traveling back and forth to Gretna doing a mini-extreme home makeover for a lady and her daughter whose husband had passed away unexpectedly. I sensed the LORD wanted me to go help with that. Being almost completely out of money and with Gretna being about an hour away, this adventure was going to cost money. Namely, food and gas.

In spite of the fact that this would deplete my already limited account, I felt I should go. Upon arrival, I discovered that they were providing breakfast and lunch each day to anyone that showed up to help.

Problem #1: Food Money — Solved.

After working in Gretna for a few days, while driving back from painting all day, a friend asked me to stop by his place of business. As I pulled into his parking lot, he was outside waiting. As I got out of the car, he said, "The reason I called you was, the LORD told me to call you today and give you this"— with that he proceeded to hand me, believe it or not, a gas card.

Problem #2: Gas Money — Solved!!!

I was thrilled beyond words!!!

Special Note: The day he gave me that card, I had enough gas in my car to get home and back to Gretna the next morning, but not enough to get back home. Another example of God's perfect timing and of HIM, beyond a shadow of a doubt, being Jehovah Jireh: My Provider!

During the week of Thanksgiving, another friend, Scott Brown, asked me to lunch. He wanted to hear all about what I had been doing. We met at Red Lobster here in Danville. With great enthusiasm, I began answering this question that he had posed: "Joey, what is God calling you to do?"

I said, "I'm not 100% sure yet, but it appears that all the pieces are pointing in the direction of starting a church."

Scott, with a look of sadness, sprinkled with a little bit of disgust, said, "For heaven's sake, please don't do that! That is the last thing this city needs — another church." As I sat there stunned, he continued, "Man, when I think about you, I think of the word missionary. I realize that everyone is supposed to be a type of missionary. But every time I pray for you, I get the sense that you are supposed to be a true missionary to this area."

After paying the bill, he got up to leave, sharing this parting remark: "For what it's worth, I think you will be making the biggest mistake ever starting another church. Sorry if I'm bursting your bubble. Happy Thanksgiving!"

I left that meeting a little discouraged but in no way derailed. Scott is an awesome guy, but he had no way of knowing all the massive amounts of repetition that God had been sending my way through all those different avenues over the last few months.

December 2010 started off in a similar fashion as December 2009. If you will recall God gave me the theme for 2010 (The Year You Begin); this December was no different. GOD gave me this for 2011: Experiencing Heaven in 2011! I surely liked the sound of that.

Special Side Note and Shout Out to My Friends: From my journal entry.

December 17: Deeply moved, what a day. Three families showed up unannounced with Christmas Gifts for my three girls. I went to the other room and teared up big time because without those friends doing that, I would not have been able to give my girls anything for Christmas. My friends did it in such a way that my girls never knew that Trisha and I did not pay for the gifts. Our friends were/are amazing!!!

Back to the storyline: For me personally, the much anticipated, long-awaited 4th Date from my Haggai reading August 29 / September 21 / October 17 / *December 18:*

December 18 finally arrives.

Right before we get to that, I need to bring up one other thing that I have yet to expound on fully, and that is The Journey. What is the Journey you may ask? Well, ever since reading that book that I purchased at LifeWay back in August entitled *Church in the Making: What Makes or Breaks a New Church Before it Ever Begins*, I had slowly, but surely, been working on all the ins and outs of starting a Church. From the name to the vision statement to the mission statement, the whole nine yards. As I am sure you've figured it out by now, "The Journey" is the name that I had settled on for the Church. During this time, Trisha's brother, Jon, had popped in to share Christmas with us. Being the awesome brother-in-law and graphic designer that he is, he did a professional logo for "The Journey." Pro bono! He's awesome. With that said, let's get back to that all important 4th date.

While I was spending time with the LORD on *December 18*, I wrote in my journal: "Saturday, December 18, 2010 — The Year You Begin… This is Day 1 of the work I love." That morning I felt prompted to go back through my journal notes all the way back to June 2010. I felt especially prompted by the LORD to reread the sermon notes from the Wave Church and that first *guest speaker*. As I reread the sermon notes, one thing jumped out at me that I had *not* noticed before and it was what I had written down on the sermon notes. I had written this statement: The Miracle will begin in the 6th month.

Now, for all of those who are counting, and I most certainly was, 6 months from June is December. December 18 falls within that six-month time frame, to be more exact, the statement reads that the miracle will *begin* in the 6th month. With the book *48 Days till the Work You Love* that I picked up back on *October 31* taking me straight to *December 18; December 18th* marks day 1 of the miracle beginning, or to put it another way, day 1 of the work I love.

What do I love? I love Jesus and I love being about HIS way of life and HIS business, the Church. After writing all of that out, just before lunch, Trisha and I spent some time praying in our bedroom and talking through all those pieces to this puzzle. I said, "Well, taking into account all I have written down, and with these dates and times coming together this perfectly without me forcing anything, it appears that we are supposed to go ahead officially start The Journey." To put the icing on the cake, once we finished our prayer time, the song that immediately started to play in the background was my theme song by Chris Tomlin off his newest album, entitled, "I Will Follow."

GOD, I LOVE YOUR CONFIRMATIONS! YOU ARE AMAZING!! Getting up from our bed where we had been praying, I said, "and so The Journey begins!"

Then this happened, not the next month nor the next week but the very next day. I repeat what you are about to read occurred the very next day. Yes, on the next day, which was Sunday, as we had been doing since October 3 (except for that one road trip to C3 Church,) we rode with our friends to Daystar Church in Greensboro, NC.

Now I know you would have never been able to guess this ahead of time, but for this Sunday of all the Sundays of the year Daystar had yet another *guest speaker*. On top of that, if that weren't enough, of all the sermon titles that this guest speaker could have come up with. God had this *guest speaker* craft as his sermon title none other than this title.

"The Journey Begins."

As you can clearly see, when it comes to confirmations, I just keep on hitting the Jackpot!!!

Cue for a Hallmark Moment Rabbit Trail

Another Beautiful Side Note: This one was extra special!!!

Saturday, December 25, 2010, Christmas Day. My family and I experienced our first ever white Christmas in Danville, Virginia. Yes, it snowed in Danville, Virginia for the first time during my lifetime on Christmas Day. The last time it snowed in Danville on Christmas Day was 1967. My wife and I were both born in 1974. What a special touch to our Christmas for God to have orchestrated things in such a way as to bless us with a literal white Christmas on this Christmas Day. Furthermore, because of our awesome friends, it was the first Christmas in several years where we did not go into debt to pay for Christmas. It was/is truly one of the most memorable Christmases with my family! Remember the theme that God had given me for 2011: Experiencing Heaven in 2011, indeed we had already started.

As the New Year began rolling, on January 3rd, I experienced a little bit of God's sense of humor. As I was reading, I came across this statement: "Don't be afraid of the IRS."

What? NEVER have I ever, (*sounds like a cool name for a game*) as I was saying, never have I ever read a statement like that in all my devotional reading since becoming a Christian. The reason it jumped out at me in this way is because I had just started researching steps to make "The Journey" a legal organization, as a Church, with the IRS. For me, this was our good, good Father only doing as HE always does — reminding me that HE knows right where I am, not just physically, but mentally and emotionally.

Keeping in mind all the massive repetition, these were the thoughts running through my mind:

1. OK, God, you gave me this theme for 2010: The Year You Begin.

2. According to Tim, you told him that I am supposed to start a ministry and that he is supposed to help me.

3. On top of that, the book title that Jimmy shared with me that *It's Okay To Be The Boss.*

4. *The Church in the Making* book with my name Joey typed out three times in the first paragraph.

5. That book, *48 Days to the Work I Love,* and *December 18,* the 4th Date from my Haggai.

Also, the amount of time that had passed, and the fact that *December 18* was marked as day 1 of the work I love, and *December 18* was within that *6-month* window of "the miracle will begin in 6 months" statement from *that first guest speaker's* sermon back in June, December was still in 2010: The Year You Begin. In addition, it was now the start of a new year, and especially because God had already told me HIS theme for me for this new year was Experiencing Heaven in 2011, I did what any logical thinking male might would do. I took what appeared to me and to everyone else, for that matter, that was supporting me at that time, to be the only next logical step. I called a meeting of a few core friends David Wilson, Josh Barrett, and Patrick Sheldon at Lonestar Steakhouse in Danville, Virginia, on Wednesday, January 5, 2011, and on paper, made a motion to establish a Church called "Church on the Journey" with the trade name being "The Journey!" In that meeting, we voted to use BB&T to open our Church Checking Account. As we adjourned, my buddy Patrick and I jumped in his van and drove around the corner to BB&T and with much excitement, walked in to begin the process.

The teller said, "Here is the package that you will need to have filled out when you come back to open up a Business Economy Checking Account." I went home and began working on what the teller said we would need to have done to make it all official. Within a couple of days, I had all the paperwork complete, I called Patrick back, and he met me at BB&T for the second time to help open the account.

As the teller was looking through all the paperwork I had submitted, she said, "Hold on, we can't move forward until after you do this one other thing." She apologized because she thought she had told us last time. I was a little disappointed, of course, but not detoured. We left and I went straight to work on finalizing that last piece of the puzzle.

Patrick was out of town through the first half of the next week, on Thursday of the following week, we stopped by BB&T for the third time with all the paperwork in hand. As we are about to finalize the process, the teller said, "Oh my, I am so very sorry. I totally forgot to tell you that you ALSO need this one other thing before you can open up a Business Account."

This famous quote from Scooby-Doo, one of my favorite childhood cartoons, best describes what Patrick and I were both thinking as we turned and looked at each other.

"Ruh-roh-RAGGY!!!"

As we got into his van, I said, "I don't understand why, but this doesn't feel right." (My conversation from Red Lobster, with my good buddy Scott Brown began to resurface in my mind. Could Scott be right???)

Patrick agreed, "You're right, I feel the same — we're not supposed to be doing this. But why?"

As we sat in the van together — we were both perplexed. We both thought for sure that we were supposed to start a church, but the longer we sat there, the clearer it became to both of us that starting a church, at least for now, was not part of GOD's plan. Not exactly sure what GOD had in store, Patrick drove me home and I put all of that paperwork in a file — you know, 13.

Several days later, I picked up the "Daily Bread" devotional and here is what I read from:

> Friday, January 14, 2011, entitled "Call it Good":
> "Sometimes it's hard to see how GOD is working.
> HIS mysteries don't always reveal their secrets to us,
> and our journey is often redirected by uncontrollable
> detours. Perhaps God is showing us a better route."

Every keyword used in that sentence was spot on the money for me.

Since we didn't know what God was up to, we decided the best thing was to gather some friends together for a prayer meeting. The night before our first prayer meeting, Trisha and I got to bed at the normal time, and around 4:00 in the morning, the front doorbell rang. No one ever comes to our front door — ever! This guy was apparently getting ready to break into our front door when I turned the front porch light on. He took off around the side of the house and came to our kitchen window. As we made eye contact, he pointed toward my side door. I went to the side door and he asked me to come outside. I politely declined. He then asked, "How do I get to Riverside Drive?" Through my glass door, I explained to him how to get there. All the while he kept looking toward the front side of my house while I was talking. Come to find out some time later, he was apparently part of a gang that had been going around, breaking into homes in our area. Rumors revealed the following:

> Individuals would ring the doorbell of a home. If someone came to the door, they were instructed to ask questions, to hopefully coax the homeowner outside. All the while, hiding around the corner, others would jump out, hold them at gun point, while the others would enter the house, steal stuff and leave.

Interesting that that happened right before our first group prayer meeting. As way of reminder in case you don't know. Our enemy does not like it when we pray!

On Saturday, January 15, 2011, we had our first prayer meeting at Patrick and Sherri Sheldon's home in their upper room. Several families gathered to spend time seeking God's direction. It was awesome — so awesome, that we made a decision to continue meeting every other Saturday night at least for the rest of the year.

The next morning, Sunday, January 16, 2011, as I was getting ready to go to Daystar, Patrick called and said that there had been a snowstorm between here and Greensboro. Thus, he was not going to risk driving through the snow. Upon getting off the phone, these words instantly came to my mind — *"Go to Dan River Church."* (A fairly new church in town that Thomas Road Baptist Church in Lynchburg, VA, had planted.) Because of my experience with that C3 Church, I was like, "Okay."

I mentioned it to Trisha, and she said, "You can go. I'm not feeling the best so, I am going to stay home today with the girls." I got up and went to Dan River Church. They had great music, a great message, and I got to reconnect with several friends and even had an old friend invite me out to eat lunch after the service. Great fellowship!

The next Sunday, January 23, we went back to Daystar. Since October 3, my family and I had been attending Daystar Church almost every Sunday. However, each day through that next week, January 24 – 29, I started hearing this phrase over and over in my mind. *"Go to Dan River! Go to Dan River!! Go to Dan River!!!"*

What? That Couldn't Be You, God!

Nothing against Dan River Church. I grew up in a Southern Baptist Church, graduated from Liberty University, and Thomas Road planted Dan River Church. As I said, I have a lot of friends that attended Dan River Church. For me, it was the fact that Daystar was in the middle of revival! People were accepting Jesus every single week, and I don't mean one or two. I mean seven to twelve, and those were just the ones during the services I attended. On top of that, they had three services at that time. I had never seen anything like it in all my days. I did not want to miss out on what God was doing there. Even though I kept hearing the phrase, *"Go to Dan River."* I told no one. I figured that voice couldn't be God telling me to actually stop attending Daystar, especially, in the midst of a revival and start attending Dan River Church.

"Could it?"

Look what I wrote in my journal on Thursday, January 27, 2011.

"Do what God says: Even if it seems backward, upside down, the opposite of what you would typically do."

In spite of all the repetition that I'd been experiencing, Saturday, January 29, 2011, my wife's 37th birthday, I was still making plans to go back to Daystar. Sorry, what I need to say is, I was still making plans to *disobey* God, once again. As we were all getting ready for bed, Trisha and my three daughters started getting sick, I felt terrible for them, but I was feeling fine, and as I went to bed that night, I had all intentions of waking up the next morning and going once again to Daystar. Right before slipping into dreamland, my cell phone rang. My ride to Daystar called and said, "Sorry, but we're not going to Daystar tomorrow. We're all sick."

"Hmmm. Sorry to hear that. I'll be praying for you all." As I hung up the phone, this is the phrase that resounded quite loud and clear in my mind.

"I told you — go to Dan River!"

On Sunday morning, January 30, I woke up, ate breakfast, got dressed hopped in my car, and drove to Dan River Church. As I was making my way there that morning, I knew in my knower that this would not be a one and done, drop in and go experience like C3 Church was that one time. God the perfect communicator who loves to repeat Himself and orchestrate things in such ways that even a two-year-old can understand it. To overwhelmingly confirm that I was indeed supposed to be there on that specific day and continue attending Dan River Church after that Sunday, get a load of all the things that God had prearranged just for me:

Are you ready for this?

As I walked in the door the first thing that caught my attention was the background music. It wasn't just any song, it was "my" theme song playing in the background. You remember the one, *"I Will Follow"* by Chris Tomlin. Interesting…

After the worship and announcements, Scott Randlett, the lead Pastor, started setting the stage for what we were getting ready to hear. Unbeknownst to me, Pastor Jonathan Falwell, Senior Pastor of Thomas Road Baptist Church in Lynchburg, VA. was of all things, the *guest speaker* that day.

Are you beginning to pick up on what I was picking up on? And His message was entitled, get this now: "The Journey Begins".

As my buddy Jay Wentz would often say, 'No freaking way!'

I mean, no way! To make matters even worse (I mean better), he preaches from of all passages *Isaiah 61, Luke 4,* and *Matthew 25* the top three most repeated parts of Scripture that I had read during my personal devotional time since stepping out of New Life, back on *September 13, 2010.* As I sat there in that service at Dan River Church, God once again had my undivided attention.

Please don't get me wrong, especially if you are one of my dear friends reading this book, and you currently attend Dan River Church. Dan River is a wonderful church. They have a fantastic leadership team and an amazing group of people that are day in and day out blessing our city and beyond with the good news of Jesus Christ. The issue is, whereas I love them, and can serve alongside them, I did not want to stop attending and experiencing all of the great things that I had been thoroughly enjoying through the ministry of Daystar Church in Greensboro, NC. I could not figure it out: why would God lead me to leave a church that was experiencing revival in a way that I had never seen before with my own two eyes?

As January 2011 came to an end, not only was I not leading that Church that I thought I was supposed to pioneer. I was attending a church that I never had on my radar. With no new revelation, I had no clue what to do next. Apart from that new cell phone, monthly gas card, and grocery card, we were still living by faith for all our other bills, and with little to no money forecast to come in at that time. I was, to say the least a little bewildered!

Please don't misunderstand me, in no way do I want to communicate a lack of gratitude for all that had been done for us!!! Trisha and I were very grateful for all those people that had helped us with each of those things. They were indeed HUGE blessings and very practical to our daily needs!!!

To help you understand a little better, this is the way it ultimately played out throughout the rest of the year. A blessing would come in, but not like one right after the next, after the next. It was more like, one or two would come in, and then a lull would occur and sometimes it was long. The longer the lull, the more I had to get creative, sometimes extremely creative, with figuring out, which bill to delay next, so that the most important ones didn't get cut off, if you know what I mean. Then when a blessing came, even when large blessings came in, it would primarily only catch us up, hardly ever giving us a cushion. With Trisha's monthly medications, that would sometimes get stressful — tempting her at times to want to push the panic button.

Temptation Disguised as God's Provision: February 20 – March 18

In February 2011, I had two friends that were in a Network Marketing Group, and they wanted to bless my family. They came up with this idea that they could create an account in my name, and they would build a team under me, and as the organization grew, I would begin to receive an income, having, for all practical purposes, done "nothing."

With my finances being where they were, never knowing week to week, I just assumed that this was God's way of blessing me, since I wouldn't be "working." Notice I used the word assumed — which means I did not consult with the LORD on this decision. Being the responsible person that I am, I could not just sit idly by and allow my friends to do all the work for me. Thus, I began to work this new business venture with them. The harder I worked, and the more time and attention I gave to it, the worse I felt in my soul.

For the first time since Monday, September 13, 2010, I was not experiencing the peace of Jesus. It felt like I was wearing one of those mats that they place over your chest right before an X-Ray. As a matter of fact, with each passing day, it felt like someone was adding weight to it even to the point that three weeks into this "blessing," I was in bed struggling to breathe — literally. As I lay in that bed, I came to this realization: "I am NOT supposed to be doing this... because this doesn't feel ANYTHING like Experiencing Heaven in 2011 — quite the opposite!!! NOT only am I NOT supposed to be doing this, I can't even allow my friends to do this for me."

As I came to that realization, I knew what I had to do. I got up and drove to my buddy Bill Powell's house, who was my upline, and I explained in great detail what was going on inside of me. Not sure he completely understood, but he knew me enough to respect the fact that, for me, I was sinning against the Lord. I told him to please completely remove my name from all documents associated with this organization. Once he said, "Consider it done!" in that moment, and I mean in that precise moment, the peace of Jesus that I had been thoroughly enjoying since September 13 returned instantly!!! I drove home overflowing with the JOY of the LORD, because I knew I had done the right thing.

Now — going home and telling Trisha was going to be a different story altogether, because my friends built this opportunity up BIG TIME to her trying to reassure her to hang in there — money was on the way, in short order.

As I arrived home from Bill's house, I went straight to our bedroom, where Trisha was laying down. I shared the entire story with her. To say she was not happy would be greatly understating reality.

She told me, in no uncertain terms, "You need to go get a real job." Suffice to say, emotions were high. Did I say high? I meant to say VERY high!

To which I said, "I understand this doesn't make sense, but right now, my real job is to obey whatever Jesus tells me to do, and I feel that I am doing that to the best of my ability." I walked out of our bedroom and grabbed some paperwork that needed to be mailed.

As I opened the door to head to my car, a gentleman that I recognized (but I only knew his first name) was already out of his vehicle walking toward me with his arm extended and a piece of paper folded in his hand. As we locked eyes, he said, "Hey, Joey, I realize we don't know each other well. But GOD told me that I had to bring this to you... Right this minute!!!" With that said, he handed me a folded check. At that point, I totally lost it, and I began crying. He said, "Please understand, it's not that much money."

I said, "That doesn't matter. It could be a check for only $1. I would still be crying. The fact that you are here right now is an absolute GOD thing." You have no idea!

He asked if he could pray for me.

I said, "Yes, please do."

He prayed over me and then left.

Needing to mail that paperwork still, I got in my car and drove straight to the post office. Being a little hungry and, quite honestly, not too interested in going back home, I decided I would stop by the Subway on Riverside to grab a bite to eat. As I walked in, no one was in the restaurant except the manager behind the counter. After I ordered, I walked to the cash register to pay. As I was extending my hand to pay, I heard the door open, and a male voice yelled out, "Do not let him pay for that!!!" I turned to see a person I knew — here's what's neat: to my knowledge, this guy did not know that I was, at that time, living by faith. As he was paying for my meal, I heard the Holy Spirit say to me, "I told you, I am going to take care of you!"

That's right, Jehovah Jireh — THANK YOU!

The month of April seemed to be a blur as well as the month of May, with so much coming and going. These months were full of activity because my girls were involved with school, sports, and church. Money, on the other hand, was not flowing in at all.

One day in later part of the month of May, a friend called and said, "Will you be home between this time and this time?"

I said, "Yes."

He said, "I am going to stop by."

As he was pulling into the driveway, I walked out to greet him. Getting out of the vehicle, he immediately began to share this story with me.

He said, "This morning, I was reading in the New Testament about the five loaves and two fish story." Diving into some details about the story, he then said that, after he had finished that portion of his reading, he heard the Holy Spirit speak to him about me. Then the person mentioned, "In light of the five loaves and two fish, God told me to drive here and give you this." With that, the person extended his arm with a folded piece of paper in his hand. I grabbed the piece of paper and opened it up. It was a check written out to me in the amount of five thousand two hundred dollars. The memo on the check read: *5 Loaves & 2 Fish.*

I've said it before, but I'll repeat it: hope becoming tangible is such a beautiful thing.

As I stood there in my driveway I was in such awe! I was just praising Him, saying, "You Are SOOOOO Amazing. You Knew! YOU Know! YOU never forget!"

Considering how truly tight things had been over the last several weeks, I said to my friend, "Do you have time to share what you just shared with me with Trisha?"

He said, "I sure do."

Trisha came out listened to the story, and upon seeing the check with the amount, began crying.

To say things had been strained between us would be a significant understatement, but as the person pulled off, Trisha turned to me and said, "I will not question you again with this whole living by faith thing."

To be completely and totally honest, whereas the check for $5,200 and the back story behind it was beyond amazing and such a HIGHLY practical blessing for my family and me at that time. For Trisha to be genuinely on board with me for the first time during this very challenging Job-like experience, was more than words. As tough as the rest of the year continued to be financially, having Trisha really with me lightened the load immensely ~ more than you can possibly know!

Another Very Important Side Note

During this entire venture, I was led not to tell anyone of my situation. I did not send out one email blast, not one support letter, even those closest to me were not privy to my exact situation at any given moment. All of that to say, every time anyone gave, they each said they felt that God had told them to give to me / my family, which made each gift that much more special. I kept track of everything I could possibly think to keep track of. One family, the Croziers, said

God had led them to bless us with a half a cow. I had never seen that much meat at one time. It barely fit into our refrigerator and deep freezer.

Looking back at that piece of paper with all the things that were given to us, still blows me away. That that all happened for me and for my family. If I had not written it all down, I probably wouldn't believe it. It's truly an awe-inspiring thing to say the least!

I never dreamed God would be this real with me!

Here Are a Few Odds and Ends

The Story Behind the Number 273 (Another New and Different Experience)

While I was flipping channels on Friday, September 16, 2011, I came across a TV preacher. Before I flipped the station, he said that GOD had told him to declare a 273 miracle. He said that to his knowledge GOD had never led him to do that before. He went on to share that the #2 is the number for agreement; the #7 is the number for completion; the #3 is the number for the Trinity, and when you add those three numbers together you get the number 12 which is the number for authority. With that said, I changed the channel thinking nothing more about it. The next day was not just any day. The next day was Saturday, September 17, 2011 – what I have not told you up to this point is that every time I wrote in my journal, I dated it along with writing several other things. Here is what I wrote on that day, see if you catch it:

- On the 1st line, I wrote out the Date plus the theme for 2011, it looked like this: *Saturday September 17 Experiencing Heaven in 2011*

- On the 3rd line, I wrote: *Contending for Trisha's Complete Healing*
- On the 4th line, I wrote: *Preparing to lead while leading (Spirit, Soul, & Body)*
- But on the 2nd line, I wrote (Yes. That line was out of order; simply hoping to build more anticipation. Without any further ado): *Day 273 of the work I love*

Remember, this is because of the book *48 Days to the Work You Love*. With December 18, 2010, being Day 1 of The Work I Love. I decided to incorporate it into my daily journal.

The fact that this day was day *273* of the work I love, and the fact that I was actually keeping track of each day, and for that preacher to be on TV, and for me to be *literally* flipping channels, and hear him only talk about the significance of *273*, and on top of that saying that GOD had led him to declare a *273* Miracle for the first time ever — for me, it was my good, good Father saying to me once again:

"Hey, you see ME, I see you!!!"

We met together that night at Patrick's house again. Each time we met it seemed to get "gooder and gooder." After what had been another lull financially, that night someone gave me money. It was my *273* miracle!

Fast Forward to December 2011

Like He had done the previous two Decembers, God gave me what was to be a prophetic, somewhat startling, theme for the next year. I heard 2012 – "*It's the end of your life as you've known it.*" Hmmm. Now, that is clearly quite different from last year's theme.

Also, during December, I was looking ahead on the calendar, thinking through upcoming events, plans, etc. and as I was looking at February 2012. A date seemed to jump off the page at me — February 15, to be exact. Now February 15 already had some significance to me because February 15 is when Trisha and I made our relationship official as boyfriend/ girlfriend back in 1994. Whereas every anniversary is special, as I kept thinking about this date, I was getting this sense that GOD had something else in store for that day.

As January 2012, rolled around, I had been submitting myself to three of my closest friends. We decide to meet up for lunch at Texas Steakhouse to discuss what we felt like the LORD was saying regarding next steps for my family and me. In unison, they all agreed that the LORD said it was time for me to go back to work. To which I said, "Thank goodness! This living by faith thing is harder than I ever thought it could be. Praise the LORD, I am positively ready to go back to 'work.'"

Each guy thought I should simply type up a resume and go all around town. Desiring to respect and submit to them, I did just that — although in my spirit, I did not feel at peace about it. You've got to remember that for the last sixteen months — not perfectly, of course, but I did my best to only do what I felt confident the LORD was clearly, through repetition, leading me to do. I know what you are thinking, sometimes the LORD leads through wise counsel, and you are exactly right. Several places I went to informed me that I was overqualified for the job. Others would simply say, "Sorry, there are no openings at this time."

After an entire month of doing this with no open doors, I decided to go to my go-to place for work. Over the last fifteen years, basically, at the drop of a hat, I could stop by this one place and they would *always* (and I mean always) find a way for me to work even if it was only for a few hours just to get a little extra spending money. When I went this time, the lady that always hooked me up came out and said, "Joey, I do not know why, but I have to tell you 'no' this time. I don't understand why. I've never had to say 'no' to you before. I just don't understand. I am sorry."

To which I quickly said, "I think I understand why, and I am betting that it has to do with a specific date later this month." That date, of course, being none other than *February 15*. Remember, while doing some strategic planning for the new year back in December, I had glanced at the calendar, specifically the month of February, and the *15th* had seemed to jump off the page at me.

A few days later, I received a phone call from Shane, a good friend of mine that attended New Life and worked at Steve Padgett's Danville Honda.

He said, "Hey, whatcha doing these days?"

I said, "Well, I am actually in the process of looking for a job after sixteen months of living by faith."

To which he said, "You're not going to believe this, but I literally just walked out of Steve Padgett's office. He just gave me permission for the first time to hire a full-time person in my department. Would you be interested in coming to work with me?"

Before I could answer, every negative connotation of being a used car salesmen seemed to run across a screen in my mind. I said, "Shane, you know I love you, man, but I do not want to be a car salesman."

He quickly said, "It is not what you think — just come check it out."

I repeated, "Man, I just don't want to be a car salesman."

He said, again, "I promise, it is not what you are thinking." He added, "I actually think you will be perfect for the job."

I said, "Let me think about it, I will run it past Trisha, and I will call you back."

He said, "Great, feel free to stop by. That way you can get a feel for things with no strings attached." Upon hanging the phone up, two words popped in my mind.

"Do it!"

But I don't want to be a car salesman — this can't be YOU telling me to do that. Can it?

I called Trisha and she said, "At least go check it out."

I quickly called Shane back and said, "I'll stop by this afternoon."

As I walked into his department — these words seemed to ring loudly through my mind. *"This is it!"*

Yes, knowing you, you've probably already connected the dots by now...

I signed all the official paperwork to become an Internet Sales Associate, selling cars through the Internet at Steve Padgett's Danville Honda on that exact date that God had highlighted back in December: Wednesday, *February 15th*, 2012.

With the new job came more transition, namely, saying goodbye to three tremendous blessings of the last year and a half: that cell phone, that gas card, and that grocery card. Time to once again become a responsible, working, profitable citizen that contributes back to society.

Before I knew it, March had turned into April and April seemed to become July just as quickly. It was like, where in the world did May and June go???

In the car business, especially, Internet Sales, the hours are long and intense. It felt like I was, as they say in weightlifting, in a constant state of doing a negative.

Throughout July, one thought started popping in my mind — over, and over, and over again. *"It's time for it to come to an end."*

I had a hunch that *it* was referring to our group that met at Patrick's house. Inside, I was thinking to myself, *NO WAY!!! You can't be serious, God? This has been wonderfully life-changing, and I am not speaking just for me. The testimonies have been among the greatest I have heard. People's lives have been transforming before my very eyes. They have started doing things for You that they have never even considered before this group. That can't be you, God!* I thought to myself, *This is a demonic spirit disguising itself as an Angel of Light and doing one of the best Holy Spirit impersonations I've ever heard.*

There is no way in the world God would want this to stop. I mean, we've been experiencing revival, not like Daystar where new people were pouring in every week and getting saved, but we were all being transformed more and more into Christ's likeness when we came together at Patrick's house, in his upper room. What started as only a few couples had grown to a little over a dozen meeting every other Saturday night. We would meet for at least two, sometimes three to four hours, worshiping and learning more about Jesus.

Remember the themes God gave me for each year. I believe these themes weren't just for me. They were for all that would come in contact with me. Remember, 2011, the theme was Experiencing Heaven in 2011, and that is exactly what we experienced. We truly encountered God in ways we never had before.

Even the theme for 2012: It's the end of your life as you've known it. Our lives were all changing for the better. I know, I know what you're thinking: 2012's theme starts with: *It's the end…*

In spite of that, the more I thought about it, the more I was convinced that, that just couldn't be God. This group of people had become family; they were Jesus with flesh on. They had truly become my people!!! Though passionately committed to these people, with each passing week, the phrase became more and more prominent in my mind: "It's time to bring this group to an end!"

Now God, when you say you want me to bring this group to an end, what does that mean? Here is what I heard: "That means you are to stop meeting and do not start again." With God being the perfect communicator that HE is — I don't know about you, but HE seemed to make that short sweet and to the point.

I shared with the group what I believed GOD had been leading me to do. We agreed to have one final meeting, and at this meeting, we would reminisce about all the great things that our good, good Father had done in and through us over the last year and a half, and that's what we did. One testimony after the next was shared. It was an emotional night, if for no one else, for me. But I had obeyed.

As I settled into bed that night, if anything, I was more confused now than ever. Here I was, not a pastor of the church that I thought I'd been led to step out and start. Yes, grateful for a good-paying job now, but I was, of all things, a car salesman. I was still attending Dan River Church, which was awesome but still not the exact match that I was looking for. For me, at least, I had this group that had become such a wellspring of life. They were my tribe! And now GOD was leading me to end one of the most amazing things that I had ever been a part of up to that point in my life. That home group in Patrick's house was for me completely and totally life-changing!

And then, when I thought things couldn't change or get worse, I mean better, God had something else up HIS sleeve. This would be something that I would never have seen coming.

Here it was, August 2012, two years after hearing those words over and over again: "Leave Now"... "Leave Now" Remember?

One word started popping in my mind — just one!

And that word was the word, "Move!" Six days in a row!

"*Move.*"

"Move?"

"*Yes, move!*"

Starting with the Who? What? When? Where? How? And Why? questions…

I asked, "You want Who to move?"

"*You.*"

"Me?"

"*Yes, You.*"

"When?"

"*Now.*"

"You want me to move now?"

"*Yes.*"

"Where?"

"*You know where.*"

"No, no, I don't."

"*Yes, yes, you do.*"

"Nah, I really don't."

"*Oh. Yes, yes, you do! You know exactly where you're supposed to move to.*"

"Oh. No, no, not… there! You can't possibly expect me to move there. I mean You're the one that told me to leave. Remember?"

"*Yes, but it's time.*"

"It's not time. It can't possibly be the right time for me to go back there.

"How can it be the right time? I mean come on, he's still there!!!"

"*Exactly!*"

"You want me to go back there now?"

"*Yep, this weekend.*"

"That's just a few days from now.

"*Make the call.*"

"Make the call?"

"Yes, call Pastor Jim and ask him for permission to come back."

"No way, come on, there's gotta be another way!"

"Nope, make the call."

So… on Saturday night, around 10:30 p.m. — yes, you read that correctly, p.m. — I finally made the phone call at 10:30 p.m. — on a Saturday night — to my former Senior Pastor and Boss, Jim.

Who, by the way, I had not talked to face-to-face since leaving back in September 2010. I made the call to Pastor Jim.

He answered the phone, "Joey, how's it going? What do you need?"

I apologized for calling this late, but, God told me that I had to call. I said, "You see, all week long, God has been telling me to come back to New Life this Sunday. Since we haven't spoken in right at two years, I wanted to make sure it would be okay if I showed up tomorrow to church.

To which he quickly said, "Of course, you can."

I told him thank you and that I would be praying for him as he finalized his message for tomorrow. With that, I hung up.

I know, I know what you're thinking. *You haven't spoken to your former Senior Pastor and Boss since leaving? What is up with that? And why did you have to call and ask him for permission to go to church?* I know, this is America, a free country with freedom of religion and I am an adult, which means that I can go to any church I want, and that I do not have to call ahead of time and ask for permission to attend. I know, I know. I've got some explaining to do. "Yep!"

Well, that calls for another much needed back story, but before we dive too deeply into that one, you're not going to believe what GOD already had lined up for me the next morning.

As I walked back into New Life after being gone for the first time in almost two years, having pretty much not kept in touch with anyone from New Life, one of the first people that I made eye contact with was, of all people, my old friend Jerry Eakes. When he saw me, he just lit up — it was nice and yet weird. As he walked over to me, we embraced, and then he said, "It's soooo good to see you." He proceeded, as casually as a man could, to inform me that God had already told him that I was coming back to New Life this month. Of course, HE did! If you will remember, GOD had also told Jerry that I was leaving New Life back in August of 2010.

If that weren't enough, he continued with this: He said, "Do you remember JJ from *Criminal Minds?*"

I said, "Yes." How could I forget!

He said, "She also just came back on the show."

To which I said, "No way — oh, my."

"Yep," he said.

"Now that, is very interesting!"

To say God already had my attention, well… once again HE had outdone Himself.

… Or so I thought. With church service getting ready to begin, I grabbed my youngest daughter Lauren to take her to her class-room. Knowing the back way, I cut through the kitchen. Waving and saying "Hey" to a few shocked looking old friends, I turned the corner, stepping into the children's hallway, and I ran smack dab into another old friend named Andy Strader. When he saw me, he looked like he had just seen a ghost. As he stood there in silence, he finally got these words out of his mouth, "I had a dream about you last night — that you were back, and now here you are."

Oh my! Standing there astounded! Well, here I am, I'm back. Thanks for the confirmation!!!

As I walked my daughter to her classroom and dropped her off, I was blown away. That was You, GOD, telling me to come back and not just to come back, but to come back right now — on this exact Sunday!!!

For you to have already told Jerry that I was coming back this month and for Andy to have had that dream just several hours earlier, and here we are both of us living that dream out. If that were not enough, on top of that, for GOD to use once AGAIN, not just the TV Show *Criminal Minds*, but the same character, JJ, in the same way that mirrors what I was being led to do, again. If you remember, the first time it was JJ and me leaving. This time, it's us both coming back to the organization and the people that we loved and left. All I can say is, "God never ceases to amaze!!!"

I was also blown away by the way we received such a warm welcome back that day; it was like coming home. People lavished us with their love. It was as if we had never left. As I sat through service, I couldn't believe that I was back, and I couldn't believe to what great lengths God had gone to confirm it all. There are no two ways about it, I was supposed to come back to New Life — beyond a shadow of a doubt.

After such a perfect setup from GOD that confirmed in undeniable ways that I was supposed to be back at New Life, as the next Sunday rolled around, I found myself at yet another Church. Yes, you read that correctly. I disobediently decided not to go back to New Life that next Sunday. I decided that I (notice that word *I*) wanted to go to another wonderful church in the area called White Oak that I had never had the opportunity to visit on a Sunday morning. I had always heard great things about this church and especially the Senior Pastor, Roger Ewing. With Danville being a small town and with me living here my entire life, during service, just like at Dan River Church, I saw a lot of people that I knew. Service ended up being what I thought it would be, and all the great things that I had ever heard about the church and the Senior Pastor were confirmed. As I drove away that day, I was glad that I went and got to experience their ministry firsthand, but another thing was just as true. I knew that I knew that as awesome as that Church was and is, I knew that I was not supposed to be there, much less stay. As I was driving home, this statement was locked front and center in my mind.

"Now that you got that out of your system, go back to New Life, like I told you."

"Yes, Sir."

Next Sunday, my family and I went back to New Life, and there we have stayed. We didn't just go back to sit and receive. We went all in, only this time as a volunteer. After several weeks of being back, Pastor Jim and I finally grabbed some lunch at our old meeting place up the hill from the church at Carini's Italian Restaurant. We met for at least two hours, only scratching the surface of the last two years. As we were wrapping up that meeting, one thing was clear to both of us: we both left the meeting blown away that GOD had separated us to apparently get us on the same path. Though we had been apart for two years, had not spoken once, GOD had us running parallel in more ways than we ever could have realized.

If you will remember back to September 12, 2010, New Life had that once a year Sunday night experience called the Living Room. That night I told God, I wanted to *bury* everything that needed to stay dead. Well, there was a lot more to bury that night than I ever could have realized at the moment.

With no further ado, I will now let you in on this little-known secret: behind the scenes, Pastor Jim and I had a strained working relationship for about a year and a half leading up to me leaving. Being the responsible person that I was according to my Strengths-Finder Test Results, I always strove for excellence but was tempted toward perfection far too many times. Never satisfied, I could not be anything but faithfully persistent in bringing up each and every single little thing that I believed he had overlooked, missed, and had not thought through as thoroughly as I had done from my perspective. I was obnoxiously observant and quite detailed in my approach to things, making my presentations — "attacks" — feel as persistent as the waves on the seashore. To say there was disagreement, well, that would be grossly understating it.

There were unfortunately a few people that believed I left New Life for other reasons, I can honestly and sincerely tell you that I only left New Life when I did and why I did because of how God orchestrated all the things HE did, when HE did, how HE did, as has been laid out for you in the previous pages of this book. Because I believe everything rises and falls on relationship, going back to reconcile with Pastor Jim was clearly the primary reason God told me to go back to New Life.

You see, it's one thing to say that you've forgiven someone, that you're good, that the ministry of reconciliation has occurred. It is quite another thing not just to sit under their teaching, but to place yourself back under that person's authority. And that is what GOD had me do. By doing so, I was able to live out face to face all the things that GOD had worked in me since my exile, (leaving New Life back in September 2010, that is) my very challenging Job-like season.

God told me to go back to New Life to reconcile with Jim. Not just in word but in deed. To reconcile, really! And as you just read, HE had gone the extra extra mile to confirm that.

Several friends were not exactly happy with my decision. They felt I was missing it this time. To which I said, "I understand." I told them I was sorry, but that I could not not obey. Even though I had an idea (the part of the ministry of reconciliation to be genuine, meaning that I needed to live it out), I was not completely sure why else He wanted me back at New Life other than that, at that point.

The rest of 2012 through 2013, I attended as many services as I could and volunteered, but primarily only served behind the scenes. Early in 2014, I made a trip to Virginia Beach to reconnect with my buddy Josh Shelton who attended that awesome Church the Wave Church. Remember, the one where that *guest speaker* shared that God was going to lay a brand-new foundation for me back in 2010. Yes, one and the same. While I was there for a concert, I walked over to their bookstore. Their Senior Pastor, Steve Kelly, had just written *The Accent of Leadership*. Excellent book.

In the book, I read his story of how he and his wife left Hillsong Church in Australia and moved to Virginia Beach to start the Wave Church. When I was reading the story, I read these words from the section entitled, "Your Last Exit Is your Next Entrance." On pages 132-134, he shared how he submitted his desire to start a church in America to his Senior Pastor. More specifically, he said, "If for any reason, you don't feel like this is right, we won't go." Right after reading this story, this sentence slowly but surely scrolled across the forefront of my mind:

> "That's what I want you to do with Pastor Jim regarding ministry decisions."

After getting back from that trip, I mentioned to Pastor Jim at church the next Sunday, as I was leaving service, "If you have any time this week to get together for lunch, I want to share something with you."

We met at El Vallarta Mexican Restaurant in Danville for lunch. I brought that book with me and proceeded to share my entire experience with him. He said, "Well, that's cool. But currently, I do not have a job opportunity for you nor any leading. But I will keep this in mind and will be praying for you."

To which I assured him that this was not a backdoor way of attempting to get a job. I just wanted to be obedient to what I believed GOD had revealed to me.

Meanwhile I was still selling cars like hotcakes at Steve Padgett's Danville Honda. My buddy and manager, Shane, and I decided early on that we would get together privately to pray before each day, asking God to bless our sales as well as the entire dealership. During this prayer time, God began downloading things to me and I started writing them down in my journal. For example, in late 2012, I sensed that I would be involved in a significant ministry on *Saturdays*. For me, this was puzzling, because at that time, New Life's meetings were primarily held on Sundays and Wednesday nights. Not only did I work at Steve Padgett's each *Saturday*, *Saturdays* were typically the BIGGEST day of the week. So BIG, that you were not allowed to leave for lunch. *Saturday* was such a BIG day in the car business that Steve even paid for your lunch every *Saturday*. With it typically being the BIGGEST day in sales, it also frequently was the longest workday of the week. The great thing is we were always closed on Sunday. Praise GOD!!! With all of that said, I'm sure you can understand why I was puzzled about being significantly involved in a ministry on *Saturday* of all days.

Fast forward, after praying with Shane privately for over a year and a half early each morning before work began, one day in August of 2013, I was walking past Steve Padgett's office and Steve said, "Joey, can you come in my office when you have a few minutes?"

I said, "Sure thing, let me finish up this paperwork, and I will be right there."

As I sat down in Steve's office, he proceeded to say, "I wanted to see if you would you be willing to start a Bible study-like group here at the dealership on *Saturday* mornings before work starts. If you can, I would like for you to start the first *Saturday* in September." He went on to say that along with providing sound equipment, TV and whatever other technology needed to make it successful that for the first month or two he would even pay for breakfast for anyone that would come.

On the first *Saturday* in September, *Saturday*, September 7, 2013, we had our first *Saturday* morning Bible study. Several salespeople and a few sales managers including Steve Padgett attended! It was awesome! We continued to meet almost every *Saturday* until I left in January 2016.

As I look back, here is what still blows me away about that season. The impact of our *Saturday* morning Bible Study spilled over into other meetings at the dealership. For example, during our Monday morning sales meeting we started opening each meeting in prayer. Then eventually, we started taking prayer requests. We also included the reading of prayer declarations. This went so well that Steve Padgett started incorporating these things into his Wednesday morning managers' meeting that I did not attend. Steve even allowed the music that was played throughout the dealership to be Christian music on certain days. He allowed me to set up a small library in my office, allowing people to come in and check out my Christian books. We had a prayer box that was passed through each department of the dealership. Employees could write out a prayer request, place it in the box, we would go around collect the request, and pray for them each week. The work environment was not perfect, but we continually heard from our customers that it felt different here at this dealership compared to the others they had been to in the past.

The way that all this started was with Shane and me asking these questions:

- What if we could never go back to church?
- What if the only place we could have or do church was here at the dealership?
- What would that look like?

Together, Shane and I listened to what the LORD was saying and then we went about implementing what we heard into our daily schedules at work. To have experienced all of that in the car business was truly another amazing life changing season!

PART II

That's Gotta Be God, Right?

As I made my way through 2015, a theme started forming and then unquestionably surfaced one day during the middle of October. Pastor Jim called me and said, "Hey, can you meet me for lunch?" We met for lunch at Rubens restaurant on 58 West, here in Danville.

As we sat down, he said, "Well, as you've been spending time with the LORD this year, has there been anything specific that has been jumping out at you?"

To which I said, "Yes, one word, in particular, has jumped out repeatedly. Transition. It's been coming at me from all directions, but I do not know what it means fully yet."

As I was enjoying two hot dogs with mustard, chili, slaw, fries, and sweet tea (Not exactly healthy, but my staple at that restaurant) Pastor Jim and I talked about that word "transition." During that conversation, I also shared with him that I felt *I had to* do this one other thing.

I had within the last couple of years read a book entitled *To Transform a City*. Each chapter in that book at the time just lit me up on the inside. I felt like, I was born for this. I briefly shared with Jim that *I had to* be involved in transforming the city of Danville as laid out in that book.

During this time, I had also gotten re-connected with a guy by the name of Kenny Lewis former Pro Football Player with the New York Jets. Twenty-five years earlier, while I was in high school, along with being my Fellowship of Christian Athletes Director, Kenny was also my track coach. I had recently seen him on TV sharing about how he was going to be hosting several meetings throughout Southside, Virginia, with Pastors, Non-Profit Leaders, etc. The more he talked, the more it sounded just like the book I had read. As I was watching him on TV, I said to Trisha, "That's it, that's it! What he is saying was what I read in that book. *I've got to join forces with him.*"

I showed up at one of his meetings, and after the meeting was over, I waited for almost everyone to leave, that way no one would be behind me in line waiting to talk to him. I re-introduced myself (he remembered me) and shared with Kenny about the book entitled *To Transform a City.* He said, "Let's meet again and talk in greater detail."

We did, not just one time, but over the next few months, we got together several times for two to three hours at a time. We talked through all of the ways we were going to transform the city of Danville together.

Kenny Lewis had started a non-profit organization called the Danville Church-Based Tutorial Program twenty years earlier. He had also just received a grant from The Danville Regional Foundation to hire a consultant to see if another non-profit was needed in this area that would basically do what was laid out in that book I had read, *To Transform a City.*

As the relationship with Kenny was being reestablished, as I said, Pastor Jim and I met at Ruben's. There Jim began sharing what he believed the Lord had been laying on his heart over the last several weeks. He said, "Well, it is interesting to me that the word transition has been the most repeated word for you throughout the last several months during your devotional time. The reason I say that is because I would like for you to start praying with me about making a transition. Although there are several moving parts, I would like for you to consider coming back on staff sometime early in the new year. No earlier than January, but no later than *February 1*, 2016."

He added, "I realize this will require for you another significant step of faith because you will more than likely need to take close to a 50% pay cut to come back on staff because that's about all we can afford to pay you at this time." We agreed to begin praying together about that transition.

One month later, Pastor Jim called me again and said, "Can we meet for lunch?"

"Yep, when and where?"

He said, "Let's meet at Chick-Fil-A around noon." He added, "There's been a change of plans."

I said, "Okay."

He shared how the Lord had impressed him to take an even more significant step of faith. He continued by saying, "Instead of just bringing you back on staff, we're going to bring two full-time people on at the same time. Here's the kicker: For me to pull the trigger on this, everything (the whole kit and caboodle) will have to come together, and everyone will have to be in 100% agreement. There are a lot, and I mean a lot of moving parts. Andrew will also be taking a pay cut to come. He and his wife Anna will have to be in agreement. He will have to sell his house there, while finding a home here. His wife Anna will have to transition out of her current job and find another job locally, with Andrew having to take a pay cut just to come. The church council will have to be in unanimous agreement."

"Special Note: The church's budget does not allow for an additional staff person, much less two. Furthermore, the church has been in a slight decline, which is the reason why I feel the need to take such a big risk. Last, but not least, Trisha will have to be totally okay with you taking such a massive pay cut."

Fast Forward to the BIG Announcement

Friday evening, December 11, 2015, while we are at my work's Christmas party, Steve Padgett made a BIG announcement. He said, "Hey, everybody gather around. I have some BIG news." As we all gathered around, Steve said, "The much anticipated, long-awaited, many time-delayed, multi-million-dollar renovation will be delayed no longer. Starting Monday, *February 1*, 2016, the renovation will begin." Everybody cheered, some, really loud, because they had had one too many, if you know what I mean!!!

Back Story

Three years earlier, during the summer of 2012, not many months after being hired on at Steve Padgett's, I found myself sitting in a managers' meeting that I was *not* supposed to be sitting in, primarily because I was not a manager. During that meeting, Steve Padgett shared with excitement for the first time about a multi-million-dollar renovation that was going to be done to the dealership and how he planned to get moving on it quickly. Right after he finished his overview — this thought popped in my mind immediately:

"You will not be here to see that!"

Taking into account the other thoughts that were *un*mistakably God, that had been popping in my mind over the last two years, when I got back to my office, I shared with my friend and manager, Shane Bagbey, what I had heard. I said, "Well, that means I won't be working here much longer." I was rather excited, whereas I enjoyed interacting with all the people, I was ready to get back into the 'ministry.' In my mind, because of Steve Padgett's enthusiastic comments, that meant I would be out of there by hopefully the fall of 2012.

The fall of 2012 came and went just like the fall of 2013, 2014, and now here I was in the fall of 2015, and it was all but over. With the word "transition" being the most repeated word during my devotions during the year 2015, and God telling me to submit all ministry decisions to Pastor Jim while I was reading that leadership book in 2014. Given the fact that Pastor Jim approaching me and telling me that God had been speaking to him about me coming back on staff at New Life at the beginning of the New Year and no later than *February 1*, 2016...

And...

because the Lord said to me back in the summer of 2012 that I would not be here to see that multi-million-dollar renovation,

And...

because Steve Padgett just announced that the much anticipated, long-awaited, many time-delayed, multi-million-dollar renovation would be delayed no longer, it *WOULD* begin on of all dates Monday, *February 1*, 2016...

Taking all these events into account, as I am doing the best I can to discern God's direction, I am starting to feel confident that all these green lights can only mean one thing.

Whereas the Church Council had to vote unanimously to bring Andrew and me on staff, I personally, only had, from my perspective, one more green check to get on my end, and that was from Trisha.

"Hey, Babe, Pastor Jim said that the Lord has led him to bring me back on staff. That means, I will be taking little over a fifty percent pay cut. I realize that is a significant cut, but Kenny Lewis said that he is working to bring me on his staff. Although it will be in a non-paid capacity, I will be like a missionary. I can begin raising support kinda like your parents have done over the years, and Kenny's non-profit will be able to provide those people with a tax write off for their donation. With all the people we know in town, that should not be a problem. Furthermore, if God can take care of us like HE did when I was not working, I feel confident that HE will provide, knowing that I am not only working, but I am doing the work of the ministry."

Important Side Note

Pastor Jim told me that Trisha had to be in complete agreement. On top of that, he said that I was not allowed to pressure her in any way regarding this decision.

With that in mind, as I was saying, I sat down with Trisha in our living room and said, "Pastor Jim said that if you are not in 100% agreement with this, then the offer is off the table." With that I added, "I really want to get back into full-time ministry, and I am so burnt out from sales. The hours are terribly long, and I almost always bring work home with me. I will get to be at all the girl's games, and I will be home more to help out. Furthermore, since God provided for us for seventeen months without either of us working, He can easily provide if I am working and especially because I am going to be back in the 'ministry' again full time." What do you say, babe???" (No pressure! Right!?!?!)

She said, "I can easily see that you are excited about this."

I said, "So, are you saying you're okay with me doing that?"

She said, "Yes, go ahead!"

I said, "Are you sure?"

She said, "Yes."

Note: Up to this point, I have known Trisha intimately for twenty-two years. You will come to understand the importance of that little fact later in the story.

I told Jim, "Trisha said I could!"

Jim told me the Council had all prayed and said, "Yes."

With everything cleared for take-off, I told Shane, my manager at Honda. He said, "Typically, in the car business, salespeople come and go, and they seldom ever work a notice. But because you are a manager, I would recommend that you give Steve Padgett at least a two week notice.

To which I said, "No problem at all."

After receiving *ALL* of these confirmations, the last few days leading up to New Year's Day 2016, I heard a new phrase playing over and over again in my head.

"*Stay through May!*"

"Stay through May?"

Hmmm. Stay through May? Knowing that now familiar voice, I knew it was the Lord, but I said to myself, well, that must mean... uhhh. That must mean I am going to stay on staff at New Life through May, and in June, I will transition full time with the new non-profit that Kenny Lewis and I were in the process of launching.

In light of...

In light of the word *transition* being the most repeated word during my devotions during the year 2015, in light of God telling me to submit all future ministry decisions to Pastor Jim while I was reading that leadership book in 2014, in light of Pastor Jim approaching me and telling me that God had been speaking to him about me coming back on staff at New Life at the beginning of the New Year and no later than February, 2016, in light of the Council saying yes...

And,

In light of Steve Padgett just announcing that the much antic-ipated, long-awaited, many time-delayed, multi-million-dollar renovation would be delayed no longer: It *WOULD* begin on Monday, *February. 1*, 2016,

And

In light of the fact that the Lord said to me back in the summer of 2012 that I would *not* be here to see that multi-million-dollar renovation,

In light of it working out with that other staff Pastor Andrew and his wife Anna,

And

In light of Trisha saying yes,

In light of all of that (that's a lot of in light ofs!!!)

That phrase that I kept hearing:

"Stay through May!" couldn't possibly mean that I am supposed to stay at Steve Padgett Danville Honda through May because, well…

Well, you just read all the reasons why that could not possibly be the case.

Twice.

Early Monday morning, January 4, 2016, I was in my office at Steve Padgett's Danville Honda. My friend and Manager Shane popped in my office and said, "Hey, if you are really leaving, I need you to tell Steve today." I told him that would be no problem.

Even though I had all those 'green lights,' I wanted to get, if possible, one last confirmation, just to make sure that I had God's permission to leave.

I had arrived early that morning, giving me plenty of additional time to do some extra reading. As I typically did, I had brought my *Streams in the Desert* devotional book that morning.

Knowing the voice of God and knowing that that was HIM telling me to *Stay through May.* I was thinking — well, hoping, would actually be a better word choice — that that must apply to something else. Before going in and to share with Steve that I was leaving, I just wanted to make sure I had God's permission to leave Steve Padgett's.

As I sat there at my desk, with this thought running around in my head,

"God, can I go?"

I opened up my Streams in the Desert devotional book, and here is what I read: *Jesus replied, "You may go..."*

WOW — WOW WOW WOW WOW. "Thank you, LORD."

If that wasn't clear enough, the verse continued in this way: "The man took Jesus at his word and departed." (John 4:50)

I read no further. I did, however, draw a rectangle around the words, "Jesus replied, 'You may go.'"

With that, I immediately got up from my chair went straight to Shane's office and showed him what I had just read. He said to me, "Man, that's awesome!"

From there, I went to Steve's office, knocked on his door, and proceeded to share with him that I was leaving. I chose the day of January 18, 2016, as my final day at Steve Padgett's Danville Honda. That was Martin Luther King Jr. Day: "I have a dream" day! I figured that would be the best day to transition on such a symbolic day, because, like Dr. King, I, too, had a dream and that dream was of transforming my city!!! Plus, that would give me a week of vacation before starting back full time at New Life. Furthermore, I needed some time to help Kenny Lewis get last minute details ready for the Better Together One Day Conference at The Institute for Advanced Learning & Research here in Danville that was connected to the new non-profit we were working on behind the scenes. The Conference was well received and attended, and I thoroughly enjoyed my week of vacation at home with my family.

February 1, 2016, I officially came back on staff at New Life Community Church. Along with being on staff at New Life, Pastor Jim graciously allowed me to work alongside Kenny Lewis to launch that new non-profit we had been working on together. After months of working out all the details, in April 2016, the official paperwork was finalized. Better Together Inc was officially a new non-profit organization. Along with being a staff pastor at New Life I was now also the Executive Director of Better Together. With no money in the bank, we charged ahead, knowing full well that the provision would follow — soon.

- April 2016 — $0
- May 2016 — $0
- June 2016 — $0

I share those details because, if you will recall, my wife Trisha was still not working due to her poor health and I had just taken a major pay cut to come back on staff at New Life, thus requiring me to raise additional money to make up for that pay cut so that I could pay my monthly bills.

Finally, in July 2016, Danville Toyota selected Better Together as their non-profit for the month, and they blessed us with not only a check for $1,000, they allowed me to be in their commercial, which highlighted Better Together and our vision throughout their viewing audience. August 2016, $5,000 came in for Better Together.

Things at New Life were going well, and with money finally coming into Better Together, things were looking up. Furthermore, we had just adopted Woodberry Hills, an elementary school in the area, and started assisting them with their open house. A few days after their open house, this report came to us from the principal that she received from all the teachers. She said, "Better Together made coming back to school fun again — the way it's supposed to be!!!" What a testimony! That is so awesome! She added that the kids talked about open house throughout the entire first week of school. Everyone was blown away, including us. New Life members were most of the volunteers. With me being on staff at New Life and the Executive Director of Better Together, we were joined at the hip in a beautiful partnership.

With all going well, near the end of August, I was out and about, eating by myself at a local restaurant. Steve, the service manager from Steve Padgett's Danville Honda, walked up to the booth that I was sitting in.

I said, "Steve, great to see you. How's it been going?"

A simple generic question that the vast majority of people answer with a simple, "things are going well" or "just fine" statement, and most people politely wave or nod their head and walk on.

But, no, not Steve.

I had not seen Steve since I left Honda back in January, over seven months had passed. Realize, Steve could have said ANYTHING in response to that generic question that I posed, "How's it been going?"

Of all the things that he could have said, here is what proceeded, out of Steve's mouth. Making direct eye contact with me, he said, "Joey — it's the strangest thing. You remember that multi-million-dollar renovation at Honda?"

To which I said, "Yep."

He said, "You remember it was supposed to start on February 1?"

I said, "Yeah."

"Well something happened, and it got delayed till March 1."

(Hmm)

"Then something else happened, a mix up with some paper-work or something, and it got delayed until April."

"Really?"

"Then somebody from the city called and said they could not give us a go ahead until May."

No way! I'm thinking to myself.

"Then, we got a call, and the entire thing got pushed to the last week of May.

"Hmmm."

And here's the thing: we had all the crews on site, ready to start the renovation that last week of May, and somebody, I guess another person from the city, showed up because one "t" was not crossed and one "i" had not been dotted. Joey, you're not going to believe this — the work crews were there all week long, but the city would not let them begin the renovation!"

He said, "Joey they wouldn't let them remove even one picture off the wall," NOW, POINTING HIS FINGER RIGHT AT ME, "until June the 1st. Can you believe that?"

I just sat there shaking my head back and forth.

With that, he bid me to have a great day and walked away.

As I was sitting there, absolutely stunned by his story, I heard that all too familiar voice in my head. The message was soft and yet resoundingly clear, impacting me to my very core.

I heard these words, "I told you, *stay through May!*"

"Ohhhhhhhhhhhh, noooooooooooooooooooooooooooooo."

Sitting there in absolute shock, "Ohhhhhhhhhhhh noooooooooo ooooooooooooooooooooooooo. Ohhhhhhhhhhhh noooooooooo ooooooooooooooooooooo."

I started thinking to myself...

If I would have stayed at Honda through May... I still would not have seen the renovation just like the Lord told me I wouldn't back in the summer of 2012, because they were not allowed to start the renovation until June 1, 2016. I continued my thought process. *If I would have stayed through May, there is no way Better Together would be incorporated much less up and running the way it is currently.* I started getting sick to my stomach as I began to think through things. "Ohhhh-hhhhhhhh nooooooooooooooooooooooooooooooooooo!" I just sat there for what seemed like an hour, dazed, and utterly humiliated. After finally gaining my composure, I thought, "Well, it's too late now. It is what is. I missed it. God, I am sorry. I see that I was wrong. Thank you for forgiving me!" As I left that booth that day, I decided, since I was forgiven that I would keep that new revelation entirely to myself. Nobody needs to know that — ever!

The next month was excellent. September 2016, $10,000 came rolling in for Better Together. We were impacting lives at the school, with Reading Buddies in the mornings, tutoring after school, first Saturday of each month cleaning, painting at the school, doing whatever the teachers and administration wanted. October 2016, we held a Fall Fest with free food, games, bouncy houses, magicians, face painting, door prizes, etc. The kids and parents loved it.

November 2016, we spearheaded a Thanksgiving play at another elementary school in the county with cake and ice cream following. December 2016, we gave every employee at Woodberry Hills a gift card for Christmas. Each component was running so smooth. With Christmas here, I was able to enjoy a few days off in a row. It was during this downtime that God took time to get my attention, again! God presented me with an extremely thought-provoking set of questions.

"Have you noticed that since September, basically, no money has come in for Better Together? There is a reason for that. Would you like to know the reason?"

"Uhhh, yes. (I think I do???)"

It's because you're not supposed to be doing this.

"Doing what?"

"Better Together!"

"What do you mean? I said I was sorry for not staying through May. Not only did I say I was sorry, but I also admitted that I was wrong."

"It has nothing to do with that!"

"What do you mean?"

"Do you remember what I told you when you read that leadership book from the Senior Pastor of the Wave Church in Virginia Beach back in 2014?"

"Yes, I was supposed to submit all ministry decisions to Pastor Jim."

"Do you remember your lunch meeting at Ruben's with Jim back in October. 2015?"

"Yes."

"Do you remember the words you used when talking about transforming the city? You said, whereas you will get to be back on staff at New Life and do all the awesome ministry things connected to New Life, you also told Jim that you HAD TO do this other stuff. Question: as you look back at all the interactions with Pastor Jim regarding Better Together..."

(I kindly, probably a better word would be quickly, interrupted this internal dialogue) "But, I told Jim everything, I kept him in the loop, and I shared each and every detail that I could so that he could be praying with and for me."

"Which has nothing to do with the question I have for you. Did you ever submit Better Together to Pastor Jim? Or did you merely inform him, spiritualizing it all in the form of a prayer request? Submitting and informing are two completely different things. I told you that I wanted you to submit ALL ministry decisions to Pastor Jim and you never did

that with regard to Better Together! You said, to him, that you HAD TO DO THIS, and yes, you kept him in the loop, and yes, you requested prayer often for Better Together, but you never submitted Better Together to Jim, allowing him to hear from ME. Finally, Pastor Jim told you not to pressure Trisha. Not only did you pressure her, after twenty-two years of knowing her, you knew from experience, that her yes, under pressure, did not mean yes — at all! Therefore, this is what I want you to do: Meet with Kenny Lewis and resign from Better Together immediately, then go and humble yourself to Pastor Jim, confess what you have done, and submit fully to him regarding Better Together."

"Oh oookay."

After Christmas on December 28, I met with Kenny at Outback Steakhouse here in Danville. I shared with him the long-detailed story, telling him how truly sorry I was. I asked his forgiveness. I let him know, that I was going to meet with Pastor Jim and submit it all to him. Finally, I told him that whatever God told Pastor Jim, that is what I was going to do. Period.

A few days later, Jim and I met. After sharing the story, he said, "Taking into consideration the weight of this decision, I am leaving for a prayer retreat next week. Therefore, I will wait until I get back, before telling you what I believe Holy Spirit said to me."

When Jim got back, he said that the Holy Spirit told him that I was to be ALL IN, at New Life as of *February 1, 2017*. Jim and I also agreed that due to the relationship with the school that Better Together had adopted, which New Lifers were heavily invested in, as well, that I should stay through May on Better Together's board until June 1st.

Did you happen to notice what I just noticed?

February 1, 2017 Pastor Jim said he felt that the LORD wanted me ALL IN at New Life.

Rewind One Year

February 1, 2016 Pastor Jim said he felt that the LORD wanted me to transition back on staff at New Life — Full time (i.e., All-In).

"Stay through May" brings me straight to *June 1.*

I was supposed to stay through May at Honda.

It appears I am being allowed a chance to start all over. Yes, our God is the God of the second chance and third and fourth...

WAIT A MINUTE, WAIT A MINUTE, WAIT JUST A MINUTE!!!

I thought Jesus gave you permission to leave Steve Padgett's? Remember, you asked God this simple question, "God, can I go?"

After asking that short, sweet and to the point question, you opened your Streams in the Desert book, and read these exact words: "Jesus replied, 'You may go.'... The man took Jesus at his word and departed." (John 4:50)

You asked God a question, "God, can I go?" He responded with this word for word Scripture verse. Let me repeat that. He responded with a Scripture verse. Jesus replied, not Satan. "Jesus said, you may go." Not they, not them, but YOU. Furthermore, you asked, "Can I go?" and HE said,

"You may go!"

You can go and you may go are totally different. You may go means, yes. The verse even continues by saying "the man," not the woman. You are a man, therefore because of these words from Jesus, the man (that's you) took Jesus at his word and departed, not stayed.

I know, I know, but here's the thing. In reading John Eldredge's book *Walking with God,* he challenged the reader to always ask clarifying questions when they believed that they had heard something from the Lord. For example, in this specific case, when I asked God,

"God, can I go?" And I received an answer:

"You may go."

I needed, as my homiletics professor Dr. Paul Fink at Liberty University taught me back in college, I needed to take "Scripture in light of other Scripture." Meaning, I needed to take that word — "You may go" — and submit it to the other words that I believed I had also received from God. That way, the professor told us, you will more easily avoid taking things out of context.

When you combine the two words that I had most recently received from the Lord, you get a fuller picture. Let's look at it again:

"God, can I go?"

His answer to me was, *"Yes, you may go."*

His other word, if you remember, that HE had already shared with me just a week earlier was… *"Stay through May."*

Therefore, when you combine the two, it looks like this:

"God, may I go?"

"Yes, you may go, but you must also 'Stay through May'"!

If I would have only asked God, this clarifying question: "Do these two words go together?" Which, to be honest, I did not want to know HIS answer to that question, because I was burnt out from the long hours of the car business. Being honest, that is the real reason I never asked the question.

But if I would have asked this question — "God, I realize that that was you telling me to stay through May, but with all the other green lights, I need you to help me. God, may I go NOW? Meaning, am I allowed to leave Steve Padgett's now?" — I believe with all my heart that, if I would have done what I already knew to do (having already read John Eldredge's book) God would have either said, 'no', or, 'no, you may not', or 'no, you may not go now', or, 'I already told you, stay through May', or, 'Yes, you may go after May'."

By not asking that simple question, and by not waiting for HIS answer, I gained a one-year education in the school of hard knocks, as they say. As a mature believer, I should have combined these two, but I didn't.

John Eldredge encouraged his readers to keep asking clarifying questions, with each question getting more and more specific. He said, "Ask until you do not receive any new information before moving ahead with any big decision."

February 1, 2017, I went all in at New Life, and our good and great God has been wonderfully and radically changing my life ever since. I have been thoroughly enjoying growing in my love and respect for Pastor Jim as a leader, as a father, and as a friend, more than ever before. Pastor Jim is truly one amazing person, and I am honored to be counted as one of his friends. God has used Pastor Jim more than anyone else on the planet to influence my life toward Christ-likeness. For that I am forever grateful!

Since 2017, I have been experiencing miracles, signs, and wonders on a level more than ever before in my life. During services inside our Church building, in houses throughout the city, and in the marketplace. The best way for me to sum up that last few years would be to share what Jesus shared with John the Baptist disciples when John sent them to Jesus to ask him if HE was the Messiah. Jesus said, "Go and report to John what you hear and see: *the* Blind RECEIVE SIGHT and *the* lame walk, *the* lepers are cleansed and *the* deaf hear, *the* dead are raised up and *the* POOR HAVE THE GOSPEL PREACHED TO THEM. And blessed is he who does not take offense at Me." Matthew 11:4-6 (NASB)

As I said, wonderfully and radically life changing have been the events of my life over the last few years!!! And I believe God is just getting started!!!

Closing Out the Decade

As I round out this decade, let me highlight one more year that was filled with lots of decisions connected to several special dates. Starting with Sunday, November 24, 2019: I found myself standing before the congregation of New Life Community Church, preaching in the church I love and attend here in Danville, Virginia. Here is what I shared with them on that special day:

My Sermon Notes

"I'm super excited about this day and as we continue, you'll understand why, there are two big reasons why I'm so excited about this date. The second one, we will get to much later. The first reason I am excited is because according to the Christian calendar, this Sunday, November 24, is the last Sunday of 2019. I believe God wants me to help you lay a new foundation, a launching pad of sorts into not just the next year, but from my perspective, the roaring twenties that are upon us.

Well, as I was praying, I felt like the Lord said, "Start today's sermon this way: Psalms 139:16 (NLT), 'Every day of my life was recorded in your book. Every moment was laid out before a single day had passed.'"

Here's the thing, if I open up my Bible, and I'm trying to find December of 2019 to see what's coming next for me. You know — it's not here in my Bible. Then, what was the writer of Psalms 139 referring to? He must be referring to another book that the Lord has with Him in Heaven, and I'm sure you're wondering: Well, if it says that in the Bible, I'm interested in what's in it. If it's all laid out in the pages of that book, I want to know what's in there. Don't you?

I believe with all my heart, as you listen to today's testimony, you're going to discover that the Lord wants you to know some of the things that are in there. If you're not in your Bible much, you might be tempted to get into yours after hearing today's testimony.

Like a good father, God wants you to know about what's coming. When you begin a relationship with Jesus, among other things, you get the benefit of experiencing a personal, intimate, conversationally oriented, fun, loving relationship with Him. Furthermore, He says, "… when He, the Spirit of truth, comes, He will guide you into all the truth; … and He will disclose to you what is to come." John 16:13 (NASB)

Did you hear that? Jesus said that the Holy Spirit will speak to you. Now, if He says it in His word, guess what that means? He's going to speak to you, and that means He's already given you the ability to hear Him, though you don't see Him. He has already given you the ability not just to hear Him, but to know what He means by what He says when He says it. I don't know about you, but that is very cool to me. But as far as today is concerned, there's the last part of this that I'm super excited about, and you'll see, it says that the spirit of Jesus will tell you of things to come. Not everything, but He said that He will tell you some things to come. This morning, I'm going to take the time allotted to share a long, and somewhat detailed story of Jesus doing just that for me.

Starting one year ago today, I was in this church building, it was Sunday, November 25, 2018. I was sitting right there in that comfortable green chair listening to Pastor Jim preach. It was an awesome day. I went to lunch, had a great Sunday nap. Those sure are nice. I woke up and did some chores, had dinner, and then I sat down with the Lord. I said, "Hey, today was awesome. Is there anything else that you want to highlight to me? Anything else you want me to be aware of?"

He said, "Yes."

I said, "Okay, what do you want me to do? I've got all these books. What do you want to tell me? Do you want me to read something?"

He said, "I want you to read something."

I said, "What do you want me to read?"

He said, "I want you to read out of the Old Testament."

"Which book?"

He said, "Daniel."

I said, "The whole book?"

He said, "No, chapters 10 through 12."

I started reading, chapter 10, 11, then I get to 12; nearing the end, here's what I read that just jumped off the page at me. Don't miss this now, I mean, what you are about to read is life changing. Daniel 12:11-12:

11. "From the time that the regular sacrifice is abolished and the abomination of desolation is set up, *there will be* 1,290 days.
12. How blessed is the man who keeps waiting and attains to the 1,335 days!

I'm sure you're thinking what I'm thinking: *Why in the world were those verses highlighted? I mean, of all the verses in the Bible that could have jumped off the page, why those two?*

God said, "Read them again."

As I was ummm,

He said, "Look at verse 12."

I read verse 12 again and felt the need to write it down.

Special Side Note: I encourage you, if the Lord speaks to you, and says that you need to write something down, you need to write it down. There's a proverb that says, "The palest ink is sharper than the keenest memory." (You will forget. So please, write it down.)

I wrote down verse 12. "How blessed is he who keeps waiting and attains to the 1,335 days."

Still greatly perplexed, I asked the LORD, "What does this mean?"

He said, "How many days are between 1,290 and 1,335?

I had to get out my calculator. I'm not fast like my great friend, Steve Driskill, with the math. My calculator read, 45.

He said, "What's *45* days from today?"

I had to get out my calendar which revealed: "*Wednesday, January 9th, 2019.*

I said, "Is there anything else, Lord?"

He said, *"Nope, just write it down."*

I wrote it down in my journal: *45* more days. *Wednesday, January 9th 2019.* Maybe nothing. We shall see. Dot, dot, dot. Daniel, chapter 10, verses 11 and 12. That was that.

Several other things occurred before the end of that calendar year of 2018. The first was, I was reading and looking at my new 2019 calendar, and February 19, 2019, just jumped up off the calendar at me. I was like, "What is that?" I got nothing in response.

Shortly after I wrote that down, a buddy of mine who lived in Texas, Shane Spicer called me. He said, "Hey, what's happening?"

I said, "Oh, you know. A little of this, that and the other." We chit chatted for a little while, then he said, "Let me ask you a question, has the Lord been talking to you about dates?"

I said, "Yes."

He says, "Would one of them happen to be in February?"

I said, 'Yes."

He said, "Is it the 19th?"

I'm like, "YES!!! What else did HE say to you?"

"Nothing."

"Nothing?"

"Nothing! Are you sure?"

"Yep,"

"Ohhhh… okay."

Having already written down *January 9th*, I pulled out that same piece of paper and added this new date, *February 19th*. Getting it from the Lord, and now getting confirmation from a close friend that lives several states away, was beyond awesome! But what does it mean? I don't know.

Shortly after that, Jerry Eakes, yes, the one and the only Jerry Eakes, called me, and said, "Let's go grab some lunch at San Marcos Mexican Restaurant in Danville."

I'm like, "Just let me know which day and time frame works best for you and I will be there."

Special Note: to my recollection, in all my years of knowing Jerry, he has never said, "Let's go get something to eat." We typically always work together on a project first at the Church and then we go grab something to eat. This of course grabbed my attention. We met and he said, "I have a question for you. Does *June 1st* have any significance to you regarding your past?"

I said, "Actually it does, and it highlights an area of disobedience for me."

He said, "That's awesome, because I believe God has something special for you this upcoming *June 1st*."

I said, "What do you mean?"

He said, "Well, as I keep praying for you, God just keeps highlighting *Saturday, June 1, 2019*."

I said, "What do you mean HE keeps highlighting it to you?"

He said, "The Lord told me that *Saturday, June 1, 2019*, is going to be a celebratory day for you and your entire family."

I was like, "Okay, anything else?"

"Nope, that's it!"

In my mind, I'm going through my calendar, and then I started looking at my phone, while still trying to engage in conversation with Jerry. As I looked through my calendar, there was nothing special at church, no birthdays, no anniversaries, no special events, no graduations. My oldest daughter Hannah was getting married, but that was scheduled for Mother's Day weekend, three weeks earlier.

As I got back to my office after that lunch meeting, I did the only thing I knew to do. I wrote it down in my journal and added it in with the other two dates:

January 9th, February 19th, and now *June 1st.*

As we came to the last week of 2018, Pastor Jim stood up on the platform at New Life and made this announcement. He said, "I've been praying, and the Lord has led me to kick off the New Year with a special prayer service."

From my perspective, there were three other dates logically speaking, that Pastor Jim could have picked, but here is the announcement he made:

"We are going to kick off the New Year with a special prayer service. It will be held on the evening of *Wednesday, January 9th, 2019.*"

There's that date. I'm thinking, "That's interesting. Ummm!" Excited to see what God was going to do that day, I wrote it down, but I did not tell him. Actually, I didn't tell anybody. After writing that down, I heard the Lord say, "There's something that I want you to partner with me on for forty days."

"Okay, what is it?"

"I'll tell you later."

"When is it?"

"I'll tell you later."

I said, "Can you give me some type of confirmation?"

"Oh, beyond a shadow of a doubt. You just wait."

Are you ready for the confirmation?

Here is the confirmation:

On New Year's Day, 2019, I received a phone call from my Aunt Bonnie. She said, "Joey, I need you to come over to your grandmother's house, I've got some books for you."

I said, "All right." I go over, and there she had several books laid out for me to look at.

One book jumped out at me. It was the *One Year Bible*. I've had one before, but I had given it away some years back. I had been sensing from the Lord that HE had a new reading plan for me as we approached 2019, I grabbed that book and put it in my car. I did not read it on New Year's Day. January 2, I dropped by the office, put it on my bookshelf. The next day, Thursday, January 3rd, I arrived at the office very early in the morning before anybody else. I sat down with all my devotional books out on my desk; I also had multiple translations of the Bible in front of me. I said, "Okay, Lord, I'm here. No one else is here and won't be for some time. So, what do you want me to do this morning?"

He said, "I want you to read from your *One Year Bible*."

I said, "Okay."

I grabbed it, opened it up. I did not go back and read January 1st nor 2nd, I simply started reading from that day's portion.

Note: For me, what I typically do when I am journaling, I write down only what jumps out at me, what I believe God is highlighting for me. And I would encourage you to do the same. These were the things that jumped out at me as I was reading that day.

I had been seeing triple digits every single day for about a year, literally, and while reading I see that this guy lived to be 777 years old. I'm like, well, that's cool. Perfect number. Then I see God has given man 120 years to mend his ways. That's neat. I proceeded to write this down in my journal:

Joseph Wade White, 1974 to 2094 I'm going to live 120 years.

Later that day, I got into a conversation with my girls about what God had highlighted to me. I said, "Well, look, here's what I'll do, just for you. I will sacrifice and live five and a half more years allowing us all to ring in the year 2100 — together. Isn't that going to be great?" Fun stuff, it got even funnier when my girls started realizing how old they would be then. Their facial expressions were priceless. (I know, you had to be there.)

Back to my reading from my *One Year Bible*. I came across this one verse, it was all about the story of Noah and the flood. Here is the way it read:

"One week from today," — and when I read that phrase *one week from today*, it just jumped out at me. So much so that I had to stop, looking at my desk calendar I took time to figure out what one week from today was. As I looked at the calendar, it was January the 10th.

"What do I do about that? Is there any significance there?" I was thinking to myself, "We'll see." I kept reading. It said, "One week from today began *40* days and nights of rain," and when I read those words, I heard the Spirit say, "You remember the *40* day partnership that I want you to engage with me on?"

I said, "Yeah."

He said, "I want you to begin that *40* days then."

I said, "Okay. I'll do that, but can you confirm it one more time?"

I'm starting to sound like Gideon from the Old Testament...

He said, "Yeah, turn the page."

I still had three or four more paragraphs to read, and I flipped from the old Testament reading over to the New Testament passage.

Side Note: *The One Year Bible* has a daily reading section from the Old Testament, the New Testament, Psalms, and Proverbs.

I jumped over into the New Testament reading for January 3rd and wouldn't you know it. There it was, in black and white, the story about Jesus being led into the wilderness for how many days? Yep, you guessed it... *40* Days!

There you go. You've indeed confirmed it again. Speaking through repetition, You're the perfect communicator. That is awesome. I was once again captivated. *40* Days it is...

Then I heard Him say, "Go ahead and calculate *40* days from the 10th. What does that lead you to?"

I got out my calendar and added up the days. Oh my, *40* Days from January 10 is *February 19th*. Yes, that's the *February* date. Now I am getting excited, I mean really excited. The special prayer service was *January 9* in the evening. January 10th is the kickoff of that *40* day partnership which lead me right to *February 19th*.

This is getting really interesting. I'm wondering what else is going to be in my reading today from this book?

Cue for Commercial

I just wanna encourage you. If you're not reading the Bible, get in there, it's the best restaurant in town. God really wants to feed you and speak to you. He wants to reveal HIMSELF and other things to you. HE is amazing and the things that He wants to share with you will be wonderfully life changing.

As I'm sitting there reading through the rest of the story, I get all the way down to the very last verse in the Old Testament portion. Here is how it read, "the water covered the earth *150 days*." When I read that, I mean, it was as if God highlighted the number

150 And the word *days.* As my mind started connecting the dots, I heard HIM say, "Yes, believe it."

I was beside myself, "No way!" I started counting and then I started saying out loud, "You've gotta be kidding me." I literally got up out of my chair and said, "I've got to call Jerry Eakes right now." And I did. This is soooo unbelievable Jerry, cause counting today *150 days* is, drum roll please! *Saturday, June 1st.* Which is the 3rd date!

Here's what's even cooler about this story: Jerry said this to me in the parking lot before getting into his truck to drive away that day we met at San Marcos Mexican Restaurant back in December. He said, "Look, I believe with all my heart because I've been praying for you that something special is going to happen on *Saturday, June 1st,* and it's going to be an awesome day. It's going to be a celebratory day for you and your entire family."

But here is what he stressed to me, "I don't want you taking my word for it only. I believe God wants you to get alone with Him, and HE's going to confirm it beyond a shadow of a doubt." And beyond a shadow of a doubt, He did!

I remind you to remember: God confirmed it when I got alone with Him in His presence with HIM, HIS word and gave HIM the opportunity to speak to me and speak to me He DID!!!

God, you are the perfect communicator! INCREDIBLE!!!!!!

I wrote all of this down on Thursday January 3, 2019:

45th Day = January 9 – Special Prayer Service to Kick off the New Year

One week from today, Thursday January 3, 2019, is Thursday January 10 which is the kickoff of the 40 Day Partnership *February 19th = 40* day partnership completed

150 Days - June 1ˢᵗ = Celebratory day for me and my entire family.

With all of this, my excitement level about 2019 just started going through the roof. The next day, I got up and asked the Lord, "What do you want to do today?"

He said, "I want you to read from your *One Year Bible* again."

I said, "Sure thing."

I started reading from the section dated January 4th and, believe it or not, God highlighted six more dates, five in 2019 and one in 2020. Today, I'm only going to focus on three of those dates from 2019 because of the nature of what happened on those dates.

They are *October 11ᵗʰ, October 25ᵗʰ, November 23rd.*

Right before I get to those three dates, let me update you on that last date from my January 3ʳᵈ reading, *150 Days = Saturday June 1, 2019.*

Due to circumstances beyond anyone's control several members on both sides of the family were unable to be a part of my oldest daughter's wedding and the reception held on May 11, 2019, Mother's Day weekend, with the wedding being out of town. With so many family and friends missing out on that special day a decision was made, not by me, to have a second wedding reception.

Quick question, I love my daughter and all but, who does that? Two receptions?

And yes, it ended up being on the exact day that God had highlighted. The day that HE had also confirmed to me while in HIS word. Yes, none other than *Saturday, June 1st.* It truly was a very celebratory day for me and my entire family especially the ones that had missed the wedding!!! Just like God, through Jerry, had said it would be. Isn't Jesus awesome!?!?

Like I said, He's not going to tell you everything, but He's going to tell you some things. If you will just talk to Him and listen to HIM, really! (Remember John Eldredge's book?) Like me, you will be blown away. I promise! My family can tell you; I am without a doubt not the same person I was last year. God, you are awesome. I mean awesome.

As I was saying, on January 4th at the prompting of the Holy Spirit I picked up my *One Year Bible* again and starting reading. Believe it or not, God highlighted six more dates, five in 2019 and one in 2020. Today, I'm only going to focus on three of those dates from 2019 because of the nature of what happened on those dates.

They are *October 11th, October 25th, November 23rd.*

Fast Forward

While spending time with the Lord in late September, He said, *"October is going to be a month of firsts for you."*

"Firsts? Okay."

I'll share one here...

Shortly after GOD told me that, Pastor Jim called me and said, "Hey, there's something coming up. It may not happen, but there is a good possibility that it will. Therefore, you need to be prepared to possibly officiate a funeral by yourself."

Now I've spoken at funerals, my mom's and my papa's funeral, but I've never done a funeral by myself. Until this occurred. Chris Wheeler, an amazing prayer warrior and lover of Jesus who used to attend our church, passed away. With all her family living out of town, they were not able to have her celebration of life service until the next weekend. Pastor Jim had to go out of town for a family wedding that was already scheduled, it ended up, I was chosen to do this funeral.

The family came in town, and we meet for the first time to plan out the service. They had planned for Pastor Jim to do the service and, through a phone conversation, discovered that I had never done one. With this being such a tender time in the life of this dear family and my first-time riding solo, I told the Lord that I needed some *extra* help. Here it was, He said to me, "When you go meet the family, take your journal from *January 2019* with you."

I said, "Okay." And so, I did.

When I walked in the room, I could tell there was a little bit of awkwardness. Right at the beginning I said, "God knew that we would be here together today." I told them how I had felt prompted by God to bring something with me to confirm that to them in a tangible way. I showed them my January 4th journal entry and told them how God had highlighted *Friday, October the 11th* to me during my Bible reading back on *January 4, 2019, a little over 9 months ago.*

Then I reminded them...

"As you know that's today's date. As I said, God knew we would be together today."

Friday, October 11ᵗʰ. God knew that it was going to be me doing the funeral and not Pastor Jim.

God knew all of that. Isn't HE soooo amazing? With that, peace settled down on all three of us in that room right in that moment. With the Holy Spirit by my side as HE always is, I facilitated my first Celebration of Life Service. God was honored and Chris's life was truly celebrated.

Driving home that afternoon I could not help but wonder what's next?

- *October 11ᵗʰ:* My First Funeral / Celebration of Life Service

- *October 25th* ??? We shall see…
- *November 23rd* ??? We shall see…

And see we shall…

As we come to the middle of October, Pastor Jim said, "Hey, I need to meet with you in my office."

I said, "Okay."

He said, "Well, I'm looking at my November schedule and there is a week I am going to be out of town, and I am not sure whether I can get back for the Sunday services. Long story short: what I'm going to need you to do is this. In November, I'm going to need you to take time…" Now, listen to the way Pastor Jim worded his request. He said these exact words to me:

"I'm going to need you to *finalize a sermon* on *November 23rd* and have it ready to preach the next day."

As I sat there, I started grinning and said, "That's soooo cool."

He said, "Why's that?"

I said, "Because that's another one of my dates."

- *October 11th:* My First Funeral / Celebration of Life
  Service
- *October 25th:* ??? We shall see…
- *November 23rd* ??? We shall see… *Finalize a Sermon*

God, I wonder what you've got planned for me to preach on that day? It must be something really important!

Let's fast forward to November 24th:

I finalized my sermon on *Saturday, November 23rd* and preached it the next day.

126

As I was saying earlier, I shared with all those people that day, that from my perspective, if there had ever been a divine appointment, today was the day!!!

Standing on the platform preaching, here is what I said:

"We've now come full circle, one full year. God started me out one year ago today, Sunday, November 25, 2018, on this journey of walking with him and talking with Him, letting Him lead me and tell me of things to come, just like He said He would do in His word. He said, 'I will speak to you, and I will tell you of things to come. I'm not going to tell you everything, but I am going to give you some insight into some things." Isn't that Dynamite!?!?

Oh yeah, by the way, that conversation I had with Pastor Jim about preaching occurred back on October 17th. I immediately asked the Lord what HE wanted me to have finalized on November 23rd and ready to share on November 24.th Because of my schedule, I really had no time to set aside to begin prepping for that sermon until later in the month. More specially, my schedule did not free up until, of all days, *Friday, October 25th* which, was, yes, the second of the three dates from my reading back on January 4th.

- October 11th: My First Funeral / Celebration of Life Service
- October 25th: *Today God gave me the message that He wanted me to share on November 24*
- November 23rd: Finalize a Sermon

Of course, it is. Of course.

You know what that means don't you? That means something good is getting ready to happen. It's going to be really, really good!!!

Okay, Lord, what do you have for everybody that is going to be in that room for that divine appointment on Sunday, November the 24th? What do you have for them? The first thing He said to me was, "Go get your *One Year Bible*."

I went and got my *One Year Bible* and read the reading from *October 25th*.

Here is what I read that I believe God had said that He had just for you during this divine appointment, on this last day of the not just this year, but this decade.

> "I solemnly charge *you* in the presence of God and Christ Jesus, who is to judge the living and the dead, and by His appearing and His kingdom. preach the word; be ready in season *and* out of season; reprove, rebuke, exhort, with great patience and instruction. For the time will come when they will not endure sound doctrine; but *wanting* to have their ears tickled, they will accumulate for themselves teachers in accordance to their own desires, and they will turn away their ears from the truth and will turn aside to myths. But you, be sober in all things, and endure hardship, do the work of an evangelist, fulfill your ministry."
>
> II Timothy 4:1-5 (NASB)

After reading that passage of scripture, I asked this simple question to the congregation, "If I took a camera, and followed you around all this week, and videoed you living out that charge, uploaded it onto YouTube and threw it up on the screen next Sunday, what would we all see?" People began calling out answers, to which I said, "I solemnly charge you with this today.

Do you accept this charge?" They responded with a resounding yes!

What a great way for God to prepare us for the Roaring 20's! By bringing us all back to our commission, the church with a capital C's great commission. What a special way to end that decade!

Call It What You Will!

While all of that was going on throughout 2019, there is one other story line that I would like to share with you. It's the details I repeated to my three daughters, at that time ages 14, 18, and 22, over and over and again beginning in the fall of 2018 throughout 2019. Here is what I shared with them:

I told them, the LORD has told me that *something* is coming, HE did not tell me what it is that's coming, but HE told me that *something* significant is coming and that it is coming soon. As we kept moving through 2019, I started telling them that that *something* that was coming soon, the Lord has now told me that it would begin this year in 2019. I went on to share that that *something* that is coming is going to change *EVERYTHING!!!* When I say everything, I mean *EVERYTHING!!!* All Caps and each letter in bold with exclamations points. What I mean when I say *EVERYTHING* is that whatever it is that is coming is going to sooooo dramatically change *EVERYTHING* that even when you're 66 years old, and you are talking to your grandkids about Jesus, you are going to point back to this time frame as when EVERYTHING changed. You will share with your grandkids that it was during this season, that God birthed in you something that has become a blessing not only to you and your family, but to others as well. You will share with them that it has only grown bigger, better, greater, and more since that time.

As I said, I shared that story with my girls over and over again throughout 2019. So much so, that my youngest daughter Lauren,

13 at that time, included a portion of the story in her 2019 Father's Day Card that she wrote to me.

As we were closing out December 2019, I remember having a short conversation with Lauren. I told her that evidently, I must have missed it. I told her that I thought the Lord told me that *something* was coming soon and that it was going to start in 2019 and that that *something* that was coming was going to change *EVERYTHING!!!* And since we are at the end of 2019 and, given the fact, that *EVERYTHING!!!* hasn't changed, then I must have missed it.

Jumping Ahead...

Friday morning, March 20, 2020. While I was spending time with the Lord at my dining room table, listening to Cody Carnes, Elevation Worship and Kari Carnes sing their newest song, "The Blessing." I heard the LORD say this to me, "Do you remember what you told your girls throughout 2019?"

I said, "Yes."

He said, "This is that!"

As you may recall if you lived in American, one week earlier, on Friday March 13, 2020, President Trump declared a national emergency over COVID-19, thrusting us into a time in which EVERYTHING changed! I realize this may go without saying, but the 19 in COVID-19 stands for 2019. If you remember, the time that this coronavirus started in China was in 2019.

It's just like God told me, something is coming soon, and it is going to start in 2019 and this something that is coming is going to change EVERYTHING!!! So much so, that even when your girls are 66 years old and they are talking to their grandkids about Jesus, they will remember this season and point back to it as when EVERYTHING truly changed.

Speaking of Change and the Number 23

After being locked down here in Virginia for 3 months because of COVID-19. On Sunday May 17, 2020, we were allowed to have in person services again for the first time. This first Sunday back just so happened to be New Life Community Church's 23rd Anniversary.

Rewinding a little bit to Sunday, July 7, 2019, just before he started preaching, Pastor Jim said that he believed he had a Word of knowledge (See I Corinthians 12:8) for someone. Here is what he shared:

"If the number 23 has any significance to you right now, for example, if you just turned 23 or if you've been married 23 years; Once again, the number 23 needs to be significant to you right now. If so, raise your hand."

Trisha and I had just celebrated our 23rd wedding anniversary and the number 23 was significant to me personally in at least three other ways. We looked at each other and then raised our hands. Then looking at us because no one else had raised their hand, he said,

> "God has something altogether new for you. It will require a sacrifice for you to fully step into it, but it will be exciting! It will not just be an add on — but a new beginning — it is something that is NOT currently in your life."

As of this writing, today Friday, July 23, 2021, a little over two years later, Trisha and I just said an unqualified YES to the Lord regarding that new thing. We are super excited about this next season because, from our perspective, the extreme lengths that God has gone to, to confirm this newest move is simply undeniable! If you thought God had given me divine direction before. You ain't seen nothin' yet.

Sorry, you'll have to wait for the next book to read all about that story. Yes, there's that much detailed divine direction pointing me toward and confirming this next move, more so, than any other move, I think, in my entire life. I am blown away, and I believe you will be to.

I guess that means I'd better get to work on my second book.

PART III

How Did You Start Living by Faith?

I have been asked over the years, how did you do all that? How could you trust that God was really going to provide for you? Especially during that season when you had three daughters living at home, your wife was so sick, and you were not working? How did you get to that level of trust?

The next two stories will help to answer that question. What I experienced during the seasons that you are about to read, helped strengthen my foundation, bringing me a sense of security that equipped me to take even greater steps of faith. Benjamin Franklin's quote resonates strongly with me, when he said,

"What I am to be, I am right now becoming."

Each decision I made, helped prepare me to make even tougher ones.

Trust produces trust.

BONUS STORY #1

It's Time to Lay It Down

It was 1991. Like any young man that loved baseball, I was going to become a pro. That's right! I was going to play in the BIG Leagues — Joseph White, a Major League Baseball player. In my mind, I planned to follow in the footsteps of another local Danvillian, Eric Owen. He played at Tunstall High School, then Ferrum College and was drafted to play in the big leagues. Although I did not have much muscle mass, like "Rudy," I had sheer determination to be the best that I could be. I already had several special awards to my name, such as Batting Champion and MVP.

During the second semester of my 11th grade year, I went to a camp called Camp Little Crossroads, here in Virginia. I knew I needed to make significant changes in my life. At that time, I was smoking, getting drunk, experimenting with drugs, and other things, to make matters worse, I was influencing other people to join in with me. God had other plans — HE wanted me to influence my friends in a different direction, namely toward HIM.

After that weekend, it was like a switch was flipped. I went from smoking, drinking, experimenting with drugs, and influencing others to do the same, to not just going to church, but encouraging others to join me. Not only that, but I also started wearing Christian t-shirts everywhere I went. I even carried my Bible to school and took it with me as I went out on the weekends.

I was coasting along in my new life until one day, I had this thought pop in my mind.

It's time to lay it down!

I thought to myself, "Lay what down?"

As quickly as I had asked the question, this thought came front and center:

"Your god."

"My god? What???"

This whole thing of hearing the voice of God was extremely new to me, having really for the first time turned my life over to the LORD. I had been giving HIM more permission to have more of His way in my life. Well, He definitely took me up on the offer!

As I continued to have that thought periodically pop in my mind, I could not help but wonder what it meant to lay down my god? I thought I had laid down my god — the smoking, drinking, and drug thing. Since I had already walked away from those things, I knew that it couldn't be that. The more I thought about it, there was only one thing that came to my mind. It was the one thing I thought about and did a lot of, namely, Baseball. Once that came front and certain, I heard it again —

"I want you to lay it down."

"Baseball?"

"Yes."

"Why would I do that?" I thought.

The next thought came almost instantly, *"To go into the ministry."*

"What? Give up baseball? But that's my ticket to college and the big leagues. Plus, whereas I know smoking, being drunk, and doing drugs, etc. were wrong, baseball wasn't."

Then I heard, *"It's not, but for you, I am asking you to lay it down."*

As I would later discover, He was asking me to begin pouring the time, energy, passion, money, etc. that I would have been pouring into baseball, into people.

But I'd been playing baseball since I was three years old. Every summer as well as fall ball and other practices all through the year.

On top of that, neither my family nor I had money set aside for college. My mom discovered she had cancer when I was in the 7th grade, and she was in and out of the hospital a lot over the years. With chemo, radiation, and several surgeries, the bills were high. Whereas any extra money went to help with all those medical bills, my parents made sure that I never missed anything when it came to baseball. I always had whatever I needed to be able to play.

Furthermore, my parents and I had already visited Ferrum College (remember, the place that Eric went to and played before being drafted.) I liked the school, and whereas my parents did not have money set aside for college, they told me that if I decided to go to Ferrum, they would do whatever they could to help.

I did not understand at the time all the debt load my parents lived under, as well as the burden they felt to help me go to and pay for college. From my parent's biased perspective, they saw my talent level as a means to a particular end. Namely, that baseball could help provide a scholarship for me, to help get me there and keep me there.

I shared all of that so that you can put yourself in my shoes for a minute. You see, for me to tell my parents that I was going to give up baseball to go into the ministry, would be a very difficult thing to do. To them, that would be a major mistake — and I mean MAJOR!

As my senior baseball season approached, I knew I had to make not just a decision, but for me up to that point in my life, one of the hardest, most life-changing decisions ever. I waited as long as I possibly could. I waited till the first day of practice. During school that day, I pulled my baseball coach aside and informed him that I would not be playing this year.

I am sorry to say this, but when I got in front of my coach, instead of just telling him that God told me that HE wanted me to give up baseball to go into the ministry, all the courage that I'd mustered up throughout the morning seemed to drain right out of me as I stood there before him. I told him true things, but not the truth and certainly not the whole truth. I told Coach that I had been experiencing significant knee pain and that I had gone to see a "specialist"(quote/ unquote), and that the doctor warned me that continued wear and tear over many years due to playing multiple sports could cause one to face knee surgery in the future. I went on to share how that the doctor advised that a person like that rest and not play.

I could tell Coach was not happy, and even though Coach shared the story with all my teammates at practice later that day, I am not too sure he bought the whole story.

Whereas I did not pass that test with flying colors, by doing what I did, I had crossed a line that day that forced me to go home and face the music. When I arrived home that day, I was noticeably early. Once again, it was the first day of baseball practice, and I was home way too early to have had practice.

My mom was *very* sick during this period, and I mean *terribly* ill. There was no good time to drop this bomb. I knew she was going to be devastated, to say the least and boy, was she ever! I can remember the expression on her face to this day. She was out in the yard dressed in her nightgown that she often wore because it was comfortable. Due to her most recent chemo treatments, she had lost all her hair again, and she was as pale as a ghost.

As I got out of my Ford Escort, she said, "What are you doing home so early?"

"Well, I've been meaning to tell you, but I could never find a good time because you haven't been feeling well, but Mom, ummmmmmm… I'm not going to be playing baseball this year."

"I don't understand." She said.

"Well — you see — I believe... I believe... God wants me to give up baseball to go into the ministry."

"Noooooooooooooooooooo! Oh nooooooooooooooooooo.Nooooooooooooooooooo, Joey!" She started getting emotional. I could tell it was ripping her heart out. "It can't be true," she said.

"It is, mom, and I've already told my Coach that I wouldn't be playing."

"Oh nooooooooooooooooooo. Nooooooooooooooooooooo, Joey!"

She slowly walked away from me to go inside our house where my dad was.

I just sat there leaning up against my car.

Within minutes, my dad came outside.

As we stood in the yard together, after I had just dropped that bomb on my mom — my very, very sick mom — for that matter, his demeanor was quite different from hers.

Where she was noticeably saddened as she entered the house, his attitude, on the other hand, was noticeably amped up.

"Your mom says you're not playing ball. Do you know what you've just done to your mother? She's DEVASTATED! What do you mean you're not going to play baseball? It's your senior year, and this is the year — this is your only shot! If anyone is going to give you a scholarship so you can go to college, it's because of your performance during this year, your Senior year."

"I know, I know, Dad, I am sorry, but I'm not going to play."

"Why? I do not understand!!!"

"Well, I don't exactly understand it all either, Dad, I just know that I am not supposed to play. I realize you may not understand, but I believe God wants me to give up baseball to go into the ministry."

"WHAT? WHO'S GOING TO PAY FOR YOU TO GO TO COLLEGE NOW?"

This was by far the hardest thing I had ever done in my eighteen years of life.

I am now forty-seven years old and a super blessed father of three life-changing daughters that are all athletic and have each played multiple sports. It is one of the joys of my life to get the opportunity to just watch them compete. I now realize more than ever that my dad's intensity was veiling just how heartbroken he was as well. I was the youngest, this would not only be the end of my sports career, but this would also be a big shift for my entire family. No more sports, period. My mom, dad, and my brother Jeff were, if at all possible, at all of my games. They were always wonderfully supportive, and they loved watching me play, fellowshipping with all the other parents, just like I love the overall experience of watching my three girls play today.

Back to the Past

As graduation approached, of course, college was at the forefront of my mind. I had already submitted applications to five colleges and had been accepted at all of them. With the last semester of high school quickly coming to an end, so was the Varsity Baseball season. I went to one of the last home games and found myself sitting beside one of my best friend's girlfriend. He was playing in the game that I would have been playing in had I not made the decision not to play.

At some point during all the chit chat, she leaned over toward me and said, "I heard that you are interested in going to Liberty University."

I said, "Where did you hear that from?"

She said, "A little birdie told me." (Her boyfriend.) She continued by saying, "My Dad heard about your story and said he would like to help you go."

"What? Are you serious?"

"Yep."

"Oh my."

After graduation, I quickly settled into work for the summer, trying to save up as much money as I could for college. Because my mom was still very sick and with the fact that community college was significantly cheaper than the other schools, I felt like I needed to stay in Danville and attend Danville Community College (DCC) and work my first year.

However, as the next summer rolled around, that girl's dad invited me to a Fellowship of Christian Business Men's meeting at C&W Cafeteria in the Danville Mall. I shared my testimony, then sat down and enjoyed a meal with these businessmen. After all was said and done, five of the twelve men that were there that day felt prompted by the LORD to give me money to help attend Liberty University in the fall of 1993.

Although thriving now, unbeknownst to me, Liberty University was in significant financial troubles at that time. Everyone, and I mean everyone, from people at church to former teachers as well as my DCC guidance counselor. They were all warning me that if I went to Liberty University, my degree would not be worth the paper it was printed on. But the more opposition I received, the more peace I sensed that this was the place. I contacted someone in Liberty's Admissions Office, and he ran all the numbers for me. He said to come on campus that first year, I would need a certain amount of money down. Wouldn't you know it? The money that those businessmen gave me was just what was required for me to be able to stay on campus that first year!

My wife-to-be, Trisha, transferred in that year from another school in Ohio, we met, became friends, started dating, got engaged and were married in June 1996. I eventually graduated from Liberty University with a Religion Degree in May 1997. The rest is history.

BONUS STORY #2

Red Sea Parted Again and...

It was around 3:30 p.m. on Wednesday, Dec. 9, 1998. I was in my office at Westover Baptist Church here in Danville when I received the phone call. My wife, Trisha, was on the other end, crying. Her first words were, "My Dad is gone."

"Ooooh noooooooooooo, Honey. I am sooo sorry — I'll be right there."

Trisha's dad and mom were missionaries to Sao Paulo, Brazil. Her dad, Dave, was her hero. He was an amazing man, truly multi-talented. As I arrived home that day, Trisha had been on the phone with her mom Barb talking through things. Dave would be buried in Brazil, and because they did not embalm, we would need to leave ASAP if we hoped to get down there in time for the funeral service. In Brazil, they typically bury the next day, but because he was an American missionary, they made an exception.

I told her, "I am coming. I will be by your side each step of the way." We only had one, I mean two, well, actually three — come to find out, we had several problems to overcome in order to make that a reality. In no particular order: I did not have a Passport, Hannah our firstborn daughter was only fourteen months old with, of course, no passport and to make matters even more complicated, to go to Brazil you were required to also have a Visa. (Not the credit card kind.)

According to *all* the missionaries that Trisha's family knew and interacted with, they all said the Brazil Embassy was among the absolute slowest in getting the paperwork processed in DC — sometimes taking as long as six months to finalize things.

Everyone that we talked to strongly discouraged me from even attempting to come down for the funeral. They *all* said, "We know you want to be here with and for your wife, but it's simply an impossibility!"

They said, "You would end up losing all that money (you will not be able to get any of it back) that you spent on your planes tickets because even if by some miracle you AND Hannah can get a passport — you will *NEVER* get a Visa from the Brazilian Consulate. TRUST US, we've been traveling back and forth from Brazil for almost three decades. We're sorry, but it's not going to happen!"

Being young and committed (I'm not going to confess a negative over myself), I was going to do everything within my power, even if it was a losing cause. I needed to be there for Trisha during this time.

That evening after thinking through several options, I called my Aunt Bonnie, who lived in California at the time. She was a Lieutenant Colonel in the Military. I shared with her all the details, and she said, "That's going to be very tough, but I will get off the phone and see what I can come up with."

Probably around 10:00 p.m. that same day, Bonnie called me back and said, "It is going to be a very looonnng shot, but here is what I need you to do. I need you to be in Washington, DC tomorrow morning at 8:00 a.m."

DC is about five hours away from where we lived.

My best friend Jay Wentz said, "Hey, I will drive y'all through the night to get you there." We started packing immediately — the plan was to go down for the funeral and stay for a total of seven days. Trisha was nursing Hannah, requiring us to thoroughly think through several things, with us being in another country for that long. We ended up leaving around 1:00 a.m., and Jay drove us through the night to D.C.

Arriving around 6:30 a.m., we decided to try and get a quick nap in because we were going to be in for a long day. At 8:00 a.m., we went straight to the building that my Aunt Bonnie had told me to go to. As we entered the building, we were met by a gentleman that was dressed in a Military uniform. I briefly shared with him why we were there.

He said, "You are in the wrong building." I assured him that I was not. He confirmed that I was. I assured him that my Aunt Bonnie, who was a Lieutenant Colonel in the Military, was a by the book, detail-oriented person, and, given the unique set of circumstances, I once again assured him that she would not lead me astray. Respectfully, he disagreed and assured me that I was at the wrong building and told me that you need to go across town to this other building.

Being on the East Coast, we were three hours ahead of my Aunt Bonnie, who was sound asleep on the West Coast. Not wanting to wake her that early, we decided to go with these new instructions and off we went. As we arrived, we explained the situation in detail, and they said they would do what they could, with no promises. We immediately began working on submitting applications for Hannah's and my American Passports.

The keyword being, we need these EXPEDITED!!!

We were there for a few hours working through all the paperwork when I received a phone from my Aunt Bonnie.

She said, "Why aren't you at the place I told you to go?"

I explained that the military officer in charge that morning told us quite emphatically that we were at the wrong building.

She said, "He was wrong. You are in the wrong building."

"That's a big problem because we've already started the process at this other place."

She said, "Keep your cell phone ringer on loud and make sure you answer it every time. She added, "I need to make several more calls now — we'll be in touch."

As the day continued, I received five different phone calls that were spread out over the next several hours. Each started this way:

> My cell phone would ring. I would answer the phone.
> They would ask, "Is this Joseph White?"
> To which I would say, "Yes, it is."
> They would say, "My name is _____. I am Governor _____'s personal assistant. I need you to go to this location and ask for this person and tell them this."

I will have to say it was one of the coolest experiences of my life up to that point. We were led all around D.C. that day by one Governor's assistant after the next.

In spite of getting off track early by being misguided by the well-intentioned military officer at 8:00 in the morning, by 3:00 p.m. that day, both Hannah and I had American Passports, as well as plane tickets for all three of us from JFK to another airport, then on to Brazil.

The only thing left was to make the trip across town and get to the Brazilian Consulate before they closed. We had just enough time to get there.

Praying the whole way, we pulled up to the building and parked and walked in. As we arrived at the counter, the Brazilian lady said, "How may I help?"

I said, "My name is Joseph White and…"

Right as I said the word "and," she interrupted me with these words, "YOOOU! must be one very, very important person!"

Thinking to myself, *Why yes, I am.* I said aloud, "Why do you say that?"

She continued by adding, "I've been receiving phone calls throughout the entire day. From one Governor's office to the next, asking for extreme favor to be bestowed on you."

I said, "Well, actually the important person here today is my wife, Trisha." She stepped up to the counter and through tears began to share about losing her dad.

Immediately, that Brazilian lady, noticeably touched by Trisha's story, responded with this statement: "Well, we've got a lot of work to do if all three of you are going to catch your flight to Brazil on time."

"Are you serious?"

Shaking her head affirmatively, we both bear-hugged her, thanking her repeatedly, profusely. Oh my, Oh my, Oh my! This is really happening.

Because we were so strapped for time, we were never able to confirm with everyone in Brazil. They knew what time the flight was leaving from the US to Sao Paulo, and they knew that Trisha was coming, no matter what.

Fast forward, as we finished coming through customs in Brazil, two guys were waiting for Trisha. As they saw Hannah and me, it was as if they had just experienced the parting of the Red Sea miracle. They could not believe their eyes. As we drove for about an hour across the city to Trisha's parents' house, we shared the detailed story with them. They could not believe it. None of the missionaries there could believe their eyes.

We were there for seven full days — they brought it up multiple times while we were there. Once again, for them, their experience with the Brazilian Embassy was not good, being extremely slow with their paperwork over the decades. Because of that, they could not wrap their heads around the fact that just twenty-four hours earlier, both Hannah and I did not have an American Passport, much less a Brazilian Visa. For them, this was paramount to the parting of the Red Sea miracle.

I told them my Aunt Bonnie could do just about anything.

I had always heard the expression, "It's not what you know; it's who you know!" Were we ever living that one out — in spades!

While we were there that week, Trisha's mother, Barb, shared with us that she planned to get the house ready for sale, move back to the states to finish out her missionary work in Ohio, and then retire. I told her I would walk around and write down anything that I saw that might need fixing up for her to be able to sell the house.

She had lived in the house for around twenty-four years. As I finished that week, I had written down seventy-two different projects, both small and large, that I saw that could be done to get it ready for sale.

Trisha's brother, Jon, was going to graduate from school in May 1999, and being single and skilled in many ways, he could easily come down and help his mom and with that transition during the summer.

When we got back to the States, Hannah, Trisha, and her mom spent a month in Ohio visiting Dave's side of the family. After being back in Danville for one week, I found myself in my living room with all the projects that I had written out laying there on my living room floor. As I was glancing at those pieces of paper, you are not going to believe what thought popped in my mind. This statement seemed to be laid out across the front of my mind.

"I want you to do those projects for Barb!"

"What? That's not possible!"

148

"Yes, it is."

"No, it is not!"

"Yes, it is!"

"But… uhhhh… But, that means I will have to resign from my job at Westover Baptist Church, sell both cars, move all my stuff into storage and purchase one-way plane tickets to Brazil because I have no idea how long it will take me to do all those projects!"

"Yep, simple as that!"

As I am wrestling with each part of this new revelation — *How is this going to work and what about that and on top of everything else, there's insurance. God, you know I have to have insurance. I mean, I am now responsible for not just Trisha, but also our little girl.*

With me, at times, I will hem and haw around something for a little bit — but once I make a final decision, it's typically final. After thinking through all these factors, I knew in my knower that that was GOD speaking to me. As all of this began to settle down on me, it hit me, 'Oh my! I'm moving to Brazil."

As I came to this new realization that my life was getting ready to change radically, my cell phone rang. It was a friend of mine, and he said, "Hey, what are you doing tonight?"

I said, "Well, Trisha and Hannah are in Ohio, which means I'm pretty much free."

He said, "Why don't you come with me to my church? We are having a Night of Worship."

I said to myself, "Why not? God might have something for me."

As we walked into the foyer that evening, my friend motioned to this guy, he walked over to us. Come to find out, he was the lead pastor. He was a hugger, and he gave me a hug. As he was getting ready to let go, he hugged me again and this time, longer than was comfortable — if you know what I mean. Yes, he's my brother in Christ, but this was our first-time meeting.

As he finally let go of me, he took a step back and said, making perfect eye contact, "I know why you're here!" (As a matter of fact.)

To which I said, "You do?"

"Yep. God just told me."

Pause.

"Ooookay."

"Yep, you just made one of the most significant life-changing decisions ever, and you came here for confirmation."

Whereas I feel that I have a decent poker face, I knew that he knew — but how could he know? No one knew. Not my friend that invited me not even my wife Trisha. NO ONE KNEW... except, of course, GOD. Yes, I realize HE knew. BUT how in the world did this guy know?

As we stepped into the service, this pastor that I had never met called everyone around, and he began telling them what HE felt like he had heard from the LORD, and he asked me to share with them what I was in the process of doing.

"Uhhhh, well, ummmmm... uhhh..."

I hadn't even spoken to my wife about any of this, but I found myself sharing with all these total strangers the entire story.

Then the pastor said, "If you will sit in this chair, we would like to gather around you and pray blessings over you as you make this life-changing transition."

"Okay."

There were around thirteen to fifteen people and they started praying these amazing prayers over me. They didn't know me from Adam. Some told me to write this verse down, and then that verse. Others said, "Please, also write this down, because I believe GOD is going to confirm this after you get down to Brazil!" After what seemed like thirty minutes, the prayer time came to an end. However, as everyone was breaking away from the group, one gentleman spoke up and said this, "And I have one final thing — you will go to Brazil, and everything that was prayed over you will happen just as was shared with you tonight, but GOD just told me that one day you will go back to Brazil — in like manner." This interaction occurred in late December 1998.

I got back home that night, called Trisha, and told her all that had happened. Probably because she was mourning, she had very little push back and said, "Not sure how it's all going to work, but okay."

Both my cars sold almost immediately — even so quick that I had to borrow other people's vehicles to get around before we left. Someone purchased our plane tickets for us. Because I had no clue how long we would be in Brazil, I ended up moving all our stuff into a storage unit that someone else paid for. Another dear friend set us up with Cobra Health Insurance which allowed my entire family to be covered while we lived in Brazil.

We left for Brazil the last week of February 1999 and stayed helping Trisha's mom through the first week in July 1999. Because we lived with Trisha's mom and because other people went out of their way to be generous to us, this extended mission trip was all-expenses-paid. Trisha did do a little bit of teaching English while in Brazil for some extra spending money.

I share that last part about it being an all-expenses-paid trip because, as that guy shared at the end of the prayer time back in December of 1998: if you remember, he said that GOD said that I would one day go back to Brazil, and I would go back in like manner.

Fast Forward from December 1999 to June 2015

Trisha's sister was engaged to be married to a Brazilian in Brazil. Thanks to Trisha's mom and brother Jon working out all the details, my family and I went to Brazil for fourteen days and all the expenses were paid just like our extended trip back in 1999, just like that guy said God told him it would be sixteen years earlier.

Special Side Note

In connection with this 2015 trip to Brazil, during this season of my life, I was working at Steve Padgett's Danville Honda as their Internet Sales Manager. If you know anything about sales, you know that if you are not there to sell, then basically you don't get paid.

Steve Padgett also had in his Policy Manual that no manager was allowed to take back-to-back vacations. With this trip being a fourteen-day trip and my entire family being invited to go, well, I am sure you can see the challenge.

I talked to my direct manager, and he said, "Steve is *never* going to allow you to go for two full weeks."

The other two upfront managers, Chad and Stacey (who were brothers) — added emphatically — "He will *never* let you be gone for that long."

On top of that, I was averaging eighteen cars a month. For small-town Danville, that was pretty good. I shared this story with some close friends to be praying with me as I prepared to meet with Steve Padgett. I met with Steve and made my presentation to him, acknowledging what was written in black and white.

I said, "If I am not allowed to go for the entire time, my family will understand. I will fly down the second week for the wedding stuff."

He listened patiently to my whole story as I explained all the details. He simply said, "I will let the general sales manager (his name was Chad) make the final decision." With that Steve said, "Go share your story with him and whatever he decides I will support."

I went quickly and met with Chad, the general sales manager, and after listening, he extended his hand across the desk and said with a big smile, "Enjoy your fourteen-day trip!"

None of the managers, including Chad, could believe that Steve allowed me to go for days straight days. They talked about it, literally, for weeks. It seemed like every time they saw me; they made some type of comment about the whole situation. The only thing I could think was — Favor, Favor, Favor!!!

Here is one final thing that made this trip so amazing: As I said, in the car business, for the most part, if you are not there to make the sale, then you do not make the money that you would typically make in each month to pay all your bills. Because I was averaging eighteen cars a month, being gone the first fourteen days in June would be challenging to make that up. As God would have it, HE wanted me to be able to go to Brazil with peace of mind and to thoroughly enjoy my time there. God did something that had not been done before at that dealership up to that point. God helped me to more than double my sales in one month. HE helped me sell thirty-eight vehicles, I would have sold thirty-nine, but one guy at the dealership had not sold a car all month, I gave him one of my deals, free and clear.

To recap, I averaged eighteen cars a month; however, in May — the month before being gone fourteen straight days in June (and the first fourteen days at that), not just out of town but out of the country — GOD showed off BIG TIME by allowing me to more than double my sales in May. Go GOD!

If that weren't enough, even though I had already sold enough cars for the entire month of June during May, when I did finally get back from Brazil, I finished the month of June, which ended up being only fourteen business days for me to be able to sell. I ended the month with thirteen cars sold. Almost one a day.

Have I mentioned how amazing God is — simply amazing!!!

Jehovah Jireh, my GOD, my provider. And yours, too!!!

CONCLUSION

As you have read, our good, good Father has intervened so often and on such a profound level in my life, how could I do anything other than trust Him. Having come to know that HE is always with me and for me, has helped me to live much more at peace. Now when I see or hear of something that seems "impossible," I am much more inclined to head in that direction, because our God truly is "the way maker, miracle worker, promise keeper and light in the darkness".

It is my hope that as a result of you reading these stories, you are and will be continually drawn to grow in your own personal, intimate, conversationally oriented, fun, loving relationship with Jesus. May you enjoy the pleasure of knowing and being known by Him every day, all day and at night.

I will end where I started with Ecclesiastes 12, more specifically, verse 13,

> "The conclusion, when all has been heard, *is*:
>   fear God
>   And keep His commandments,
>   because this *applies* to every person."

I declare, you'll be so very glad you did!

NOTES

Introduction

1. Ecclesiastes 12:12 NASB 1995

2. www.google.com How many books are there in the world?

3. Rob Bell, *How to be HERE* Page 140

4. Max Lucado, *You Can Be EVERYTHING God Wants You to Be* Page 43

5. Albert Einstein Quote

6. Morgan Harper Nichols Quote from a Blog

7. Revelation 19:10 NASB 1995

8. Revelation 12:11 NASB 1995

Part I

1. *Streams in the Desert* August 23 Page 322 Hebrews 11:8 NIV

2. *Streams in the Desert* August 23 Page 322-323 from Days of Heaven upon Earth

3. *Streams in the Desert* August 23 Page 323

4. C.H. Spurgeon Quote — "Fair weather faith is not faith at all"

5. Hebrews 11:8 NIV

6. Francis Chan's Last Sermon at Cornerstone Church — Youtube

7. Bruce Tulgan, *It's Okay to be the Boss*

8. Ben Arment, *Church in the Making What Makes or Breaks a New Church Before it Starts* Foreword: "Red Rover... send Joey right over!"

9. Diff'rent Strokes Actor Arnold Jackson famous line, played by Gary Coleman

10. *Streams in the Desert*, Page 347

11. My Utmost for His Highest Title Page — "After Surrender — Then What" from September 13, Page Number Not Provided

12. Luke 4:1 NASB 1995

13. *Streams in the Desert* Page 362-363 I Kings 19:12 NIV George Matheson

14. Bill Hybels, *The Power of a Whisper*

15. *Streams in the Desert*, Poem on Page 363

16. Life Application Study Bible New Living Translation: Book of Haggai Pages 1364-1366

17. John Eldredge, *Walking with God*

18. Isaiah 61 NASB 1995

19. Luke 4:17-20 NASB 1995

20. Matthew 25 NASB 1995

21. Criminal Minds TV Show "JJ's Goodbye and Last Scene"

22. Genesis 22:14 NASB 1995

23. North Point Community Church "Game Plan: Discover God's Will for your Next Step" Sermon Series by Andy Stanley & Jeff Henderson

24. *Streams in the Desert*, October 19 Page 395 A.B. Simpson

25. *Streams in the Desert*, October 23 Reading, Pages 400

26. *Streams in the Desert*, October 5 I Kings 17:7 NIV Reading, Pages 376 F.B. Meyer

27. Dave Ramsey, *Total Money Makeover*

28. Matthew 16:9-11 NASB 1995

29. Dan Miller, *48 Days to The Work You Love*

30. *Streams in the Desert* November 1 Reading from Daily Devotional Commentary

31. *Streams in the Desert* November 1 Reading, Poem An hour of waiting! F.M.N

32. 2 Thessalonians 3:10 — "If you don't work, you don't eat."

33. Chris Tomlin Song, "I Will Follow"

34. *Grace For the Moment*: By Max Lucado Worthless Worry "Don't be afraid of the IRS"

35. Daily Bread Reading from Friday, January 14, 2011. "Call it Good"

36. Personal Journal Entry Thursday January 27, 2011

37. Matthew 14:13-21. 5 Loaves and 2 Fish

38. Criminal Minds TV Show "JJ Returns," August 2012

39. Steve Kelly, *The Accent of Leadership: Words Matter*

Part II

1. Eric Swanson and Sam Williams, *To Transform a City*

2. *Streams in the Desert*, Page 17, January 4 Reading

3. *Streams in the Desert*, Page 17, January 4 Reading

4. John Eldredge, *Walking with God*

5. Matthew 11:4-6 NASB 1995

6. Psalms 139:16 NLT

7. John 16:13 NASB 1995

8. Daniel 10-12 NASB 1995

9. Chinese Proverb

10. *One Year Bible*

11. 2 Timothy 4:1-5 NASB 1995

12. President Trump's Announcement: National State of Emergency

Bonus Story #1

1. Benjamin Franklin Quote www.azquites.com

Conclusion

1. Joshua Leeland, "Way Maker"
2. Ecclesiastes 12:13 NASB 1995

CPSIA information can be obtained
at www.ICGtesting.com
Printed in the USA
BVHW040311210322
631575BV00004B/11